T0198521

EQUIPPED
For
HOLINESS

Dr. Shirley F. Thurman

WESTBOW
PRESS®
A DIVISION OF THOMAS NELSON
& ZONDERVAN

Unless otherwise indicated, all Scripture taken from the New King James Version®. Copyright © 1982 by Thomas Nelson. Used by permission. All rights reserved.

Scripture quotations marked (NIV) are taken from the Holy Bible, New International Version®, NIV®. Copyright © 1973, 1978, 1984, 2011 by Biblica, Inc.™ Used by permission of Zondervan. All rights reserved worldwide. www. zondervan.com The "NIV" and "New International Version" are trademarks registered in the United States Patent and Trademark Office by Biblica, Inc.™

Scripture quotations marked (AMP) are taken from the Amplified Bible, Copyright © 1954, 1958, 1962, 1964, 1965, 1987 by The Lockman Foundation. Used by permission.

Scripture quotations marked (KJV) are taken from the King James Version of the Bible.

Scripture quotations marked (NLT) are taken from the Holy Bible, New Living Translation, copyright ©1996, 2004, 2015 by Tyndale House Foundation. Used by permission of Tyndale House Publishers, Inc., Carol Stream, Illinois 60188. All rights reserved.

WestBow Press books may be ordered through booksellers or by contacting:

WestBow Press
A Division of Thomas Nelson & Zondervan
1663 Liberty Drive
Bloomington, IN 47403
www.westbowpress.com
1 (866) 928-1240

ISBN: 978-1-9736-6777-3 (sc)
ISBN: 978-1-9736-6778-0 (hc)
ISBN: 978-1-9736-6776-6 (e)

Library of Congress Control Number: 2019908970

Print information available on the last page.

WestBow Press rev. date: 07/16/2019

CONTENTS

1

CHAPTER

Foundations

There is an old story among horsemen concerning the practice of buying horses in Arabia many years ago. When someone was interested in a particular horse, he would be escorted by the leader of the tribe (owner of the horse) inside the master's tent while the horse would be led outside the tent. At this point, the side of the tent would be slowly lifted to show the horse's feet. The interested party was then allowed to examine the feet carefully. When he was satisfied, the side of the tent would be lifted higher, and he would be invited to check out the legs. When he was content that the horse was sound of leg and foot, he would then be allowed to view the animal in its entirety.

There are several reasons for this. Living in desert areas, a horse had to have good feet and legs. Without them, the person who depended on horses for survival could be put in physical jeopardy if the horse became lame. Without strong feet and legs, the horses would never be able to travel the long distances required of them, nor would they be able to carry or pull the loads on which the people depended. They also would not be fast or swift in battle. A horse is beautiful in form and strength. It is easy to be led astray by the outward appearance and completely miss a problem with legs or feet. Therefore, the legs and feet were of primary importance. That is the reason they were viewed first.

What could this possibly have to do with our lives as Christians? More than meets the eye. If, for example, our foundation is faulty, then so is everything else. A horse's foundation means his feet and legs. Without them, he is not a horse at all and not good for much else, regardless of how pretty or appealing the horse might be. It is the same with our faith. If the foundation of our faith is not firmly grounded in God's Word, then we too might be in jeopardy.

Salvation is the main theme of the Bible, as it is the story God's redemptive history. One could even say the Bible is the story of salvation and be correct.[1] This salvation is the most important thing in our lives. It is primary; without it, we have nothing. There would be no life, no hope, no peace, and no future. There would be nothing. From Genesis to Revelation, the theme is God's salvific[2] grace being brought down to humans. We should take it seriously. Not only do our lives here depend on it, but also our eternal destination. As Christians, this is our foundation. It is of the utmost significance that we discern the true from the false.

So much of what passes for Christianity is grounded in feelings, experiences, false teaching, or new revelation. We need to know as Christians that we are indeed on the right path, for the scriptures tell us "there is a path that seems right to man, but the end thereof is destruction" (Prv 14:12). As Dr. Walter Martin was so fond of saying, "As Christians it is not enough to know what we believe, we must also know why we believe it."[3]

[1]   Max Lucado and Randy Frazee, *The Story. NIV* (Grand Rapids, MI: Zondervan, 2011), forward, vii.
[2]   David S. Dockery, Trent C. Butler, Christopher L. Church, et al., *Holman Bible Handbook* (Nashville, TN: Holman Bible Publishers, 1992), Logos.
[3]   Dr. Walter Martin, *Kingdom of the Cults* (Bethany House, Grand Rapids, MI, 1977).

We are now living in a world of biblical illiteracy, even within the churches. How can we stand when things get tough if we are not even aware of what we believe? How can we know what pleases God if we don't know what the Bible says? How do we know when to flee evil or to do what is right if we haven't studied His Word? The Bible is God's Word to us. It is not just for first-century believers but for believers today as well. How would we feel if we sent a letter to loved ones to tell them that we love them and to warn them about what they need to do to stay safe in dangerous times, only to have them receive it and then never open it and read it? Would we be disappointed? Concerned? Of course we would.

When a person undertakes the task of building a house, the foundation has to be set on solid ground. In the same manner, our foundations should not be built on shifting sands (such as feelings, experience, false teaching, or new revelations). They should be built firmly on God's Word (Mt 7:24–27). Those shifting sands move just like the large dunes in the Sahara or like large waves in the ocean. One might think one is on firm ground only to find the ground shifts or the water moves, and one is in midair with nowhere to go but down. There is nothing underneath for support that is not also moving. This is evident in our culture today as it is literally shifting beneath our feet.[4] It seems to be more of an upheaval than merely a shift.

When we build on bedrock, our foundation is sure, and we will not be moved, even in the worst of storms. This is because it is real, unmovable, and solid. It is a strong anchor. Jesus Himself is referred to as the cornerstone for the building to be built upon (1 Pt 2:4–8). For the Christian that bedrock is Christ and the Bible (the Old Testament in Jesus's day), which was and is steadfast and sure. Even Jesus Himself said, "Heaven and Earth would pass away before even one jot or tittle was removed from it" (Mt 5:18, Lk 16:17).

---

[4]   Nancy Pearcy, *Total Truth* (Wheaton, IL: Crossway Books, 2005), 23.

So what is it exactly that we need to know as Christians? Actually, it's quite simple. First, we need to know that we are sinners. Second, we need to know that Jesus is the Savior. It really is that easy.[5] The gospel was meant to be so uncomplicated that even the simple would understand it. Humans are the ones who take it and try to make it much more difficult than it is. According to Nelson:

> In the Gospel the way of life is made so plain that the feeblest intellect can understand how to approach God, and the wisest of earth cannot fathom the depth of God's wisdom as seen in the divine plan of salvation (Rom 11:33–36).[6]

It is not necessary for a person to understand all there is to know about theology, soteriology, angelology, pneumatology, sanctification, Christology, eschatology, apologetics, or any other *ology* to become a Christian. Those are great things to study and learn, but they are not essential to come to Christ and have your life transformed. As Peter Kreeft so eloquently put it: "When we die there will be no theology exams for entrance to heaven."[7]

The truth of the matter is that it is much harder resisting Christ than coming to Him and following. But how do we learn to follow Him and live for Him in a way that is pleasing to Him after salvation has taken place?

What exactly does it mean to be saved? Saved from what? We hear this term so often. Rather than get into a big discussion of soteriology (the study of salvation), let's just be as brief as possible. After we come to the conclusion (by the convicting power of the

---

5   Myer Pearlman, *Knowing the Doctrines of the Bible* (Springfield, MO: Gospel Publishing House, 1937), 20.

6   P. C. Nelson, *Bible Doctrines* (Springfield, MO: Gospel Publishing House), 19.

7   Peter Kreeft and Ronald K. Tacelli, *Handbook of Christian Apologetics* (Downers Grove, IL: Intervarsity Press, 1994), 326.

Holy Spirit) that we are indeed sinners and that there is nothing we can do to fix that, we begin to look for a savior who can fix things for us. God already made provision for that back at the very beginning of time (2 Tm 1:9). He did this by sending Christ to save us by His death on the cross for our sins. He did this so we could be reconciled to a Holy God, through Jesus Christ. Jesus's main purpose for coming to earth was to save sinners (1 Tm 1:15). His primary purpose was not to do miracles, teach, or heal. He came first and foremost to seek and save those who were lost (Lk 19:10 NIV). Yes, He did teach, He did do miracles, and He did heal people while He was here. However, that wasn't His main objective. He did those out of compassion and love for the people He created. He still does so today.[8]

By repenting and placing our faith or trust in Jesus to save us from that sin, we too can be saved. This is called grace. It comes from God and His love for humankind, and all we need to do is believe it (Jn 1:12, 3:16).

It is vital that we comprehend what salvation is and how it manifests itself. People call themselves Christians for many different reasons. Some do so because their parents were Christian. Others do so because they live in America. Others might because they attend church regularly. Some might even be very religious. Many think somehow their salvation is due to their behavior or following certain rules to be saved. Well, none of these things save us. It is by God's grace alone that we are saved *(sola gratia)*. And we receive that grace by faith alone *(sola fide)*.[9]

Now there are several phases that we go through in our salvation experience. The primary ones that we are going to address are repentance, justification, and regeneration. These are necessary for a simple understanding of the process of conversion. These all occur

---

8   Dr. Charles Stanley, *In Touch Ministries* broadcast.
9   John F. MacArthur Jr., *Rediscovering Expository Preaching* (Dallas, TX: Word, 1992), 47.

simultaneously at the point of repentance and faith. Therefore, it isn't necessary to discuss all the other phases at this juncture.

Repentance

We hear so much today about accepting Jesus. What does this mean exactly? More often than not, this is where we come forward at a meeting to pray the sinner's prayer, and we then are saved. Although we do "accept" Jesus into our hearts or make a decision to follow Christ, at some point, we all express something like the sinner's prayer. Many times that is all there is. Salvation is so much more than just a repeated prayer, confession, or church attendance. Salvation isn't a club that one joins, by accepting the policy of the club bylaws. Genuine salvation produces a change—quite often a dramatic one—as the Holy Spirit begins a work in us.

Very seldom do we hear a message of repentance today, and yet without repentance how can there be salvation? Oden would ask, "How can we know we need to repent unless we first understand that we are sinners and that we are lost?"[10] This is a very unpopular concept in our politically correct culture, where everything is relative, and there are no absolutes of right or wrong. We need to understand that in the Bible there are ultimately two types of people. There are those who are saved, and there are those who are lost.

Each one of us falls into one category or the other. If people do not repent of their sin and place their trust in Christ, then they are like sheep without a shepherd. They are lost. It does not mean that they are all necessarily bad people. Some of them may be very good, creative, imaginative, hard-working, loyal, and wonderful parents or neighbors. Nonetheless they are sheep without a shepherd. A sheep on its own will not survive. Roberts would respond by saying, "Preaching the great doctrines of the Bible divides the sheep from

---

[10] Thomas C. Oden, *Classic Christianity* (Broadway, NY: Harper Collins, 1992), 562.

the goats."[11] Sheep are helpless without a shepherd, whereas goats are not. Either people have been saved by the blood of Jesus Christ, or they are still lost in their sin.

So what exactly does repentance mean and why do we need it? It means to turn away from. A good way to think of it is as a U-turn.[12] A person is headed down the freeway and he or she comes to a place where there is a realization of heading in the wrong direction. As such, the person turns around and then proceeds in the appropriate direction.

Repentance is also a godly sorrow for the way we have lived and the sins we have committed, knowingly or unknowingly, and a strong desire to be free of them and to turn away.[13]

There are things that repentance is not. It is not just a sorrow of being caught in some wrongdoing and fearing punishment. This just means that a person is sorry for being caught. That does not mean that a person is really sick of it and wants to stop. This type of sorrow means the minute a person is released that person will most often go right back to doing that for which he or she was caught. This sorrow is not repentance, nor does it lead to repentance. A person can feel much sorrow or guilt or remorse over his or her choices and behavior, and it doesn't lead the person to repentance. Such was the case of Judas in Matthew 27:3–5 (NIV). Judas had remorse over what he had done. He could have gone to Jesus and repented and asked for forgiveness. However, he decided to commit suicide instead.[14]

In contrast, a godly sorry is a sickness of the soul over sin and the way one is living. A person has to decide to turn away and

---

[11]   Richard Owen Roberts, *Repentance: The First Word of the Gospel* (Wheaton, IL: Crossway, 2002), 14.

[12]   John Lyndon, *From Sacrifice to Sacrament: Repentance in A Christian context.* (Nanham, NY: Rowan & Littlefield, 1977), 46. Logos.

[13]   R. C. Sproul, *What Is Repentance* (Sanford, FL: Reformation Trust, 2014), 2–3.

[14]   Michael Cocoris. *Repentance: the Most Misunderstood Word in the Bible*(Milwaukee, WI: Grace Gospel, 1982), 7.

renounce sin and leave it behind. This is repentance. So we come to God ashamed, broken, disillusioned, disappointed, and worn down with our guilt and our hurts. We are fully aware of the sin that has us bound. We believe Jesus to be the savior and simply confess our sin and ask Him to forgive us. How beautifully simple is that? According to Utley, "The definition of both the Hebrew and Greek terms are required to grasp the full meaning of repentance. The Hebrew demands a change of action. While the Greek demands a change of mind. The saved person receives a new mind and heart. He thinks differently and lives differently."[15]

On the subject of belief, we should clarify that this is an active belief not passive. Many people "believe" in Jesus, and it never goes any further. They believe He lived and died; they might even believe He rose from the dead and even believe that He is the Savior or God and still not have believing faith. James 2:19 (NIV) says, "You believe that there is one God? Good! Even the demons believe that and shudder with fear." So when speaking of believing let us dispense with a passive belief and grasp an active faith.[16]

Abraham and Noah were both listed among the righteous. Why? It is because it says they believed God and acted according to what they believed. Genuine faith is built upon our belief and must be a functional faith.

Suppose someone informed people that a bad flood was coming to their area and that people should prepare. Let's further suppose the people claimed to heed the warning. Yet when they went home, they did nothing. In this scenario they lost everything—loved ones, possessions. Everything wiped out by the flood. Did they really believe? On the other hand, suppose they believed what was said and then went home and packed up their loved ones and took them all to

---

[15]   Robert James Utley, *Vol 9, Paul's Fourth Missionary Journey: I Timothy, Titus, II Timothy, Study Guide Commentary Series* (Marshall, TX: Bible Lessons International, 2000), 158. Logos.

[16]   William G. T. Shedd. *Dogmatic Theology,* 3rd ed. (Phillipsburg, NJ: P & R Publishing, 2003), 787.

a safer place. Which of the two could we say really believed? This is how it is with the word *believe* in the Bible. It is not a passive word but an active one. If we truly *believe* what the Bible says, our actions should back that up. What we truly believe affects everything we do or think. Mark 1:15 says, "Repent ye, and believe in the gospel."

"True repentance requires the abandonment of the life of sin (Clement of Alexander., Who is the Rich Man That Is Being Saved? "It leads to reshaping of behavior" (Calvin, Inst. 3.4).[17] Oden would continue with, "Repentance is an act aimed at the root of sin, not just a trimming of leaves and branches, but going straight to the root."[18]

J. C. Ryle had this to say of repentance: "A thorough change of man's natural heart upon the subject of sin. When our heart is changed by the Holy Spirit and this natural love of sin is cast out, then that change takes place which the word of God calls repentance."[19]

Justification

This is where grace really comes into view. If we are sincere in our repentance, He will not only forgive us of those sins, but cleanse us of all unrighteousness and put His Spirit to live inside of us from that day forward.

This repentance leads to justification before God. It is the work of redemption in which God then declares us not guilty. It is a legal term meaning that we are acquitted. Our sins are no longer applied to our account but erased. Our account has been settled.[20] Jesus has paid the price for our admission into His kingdom. He did this

---

[17] Oden, 573.

[18] Oden, 575.

[19] J. C. Ryle, *Holiness: Its Nature, Hindrances, Difficulties, and Roots.* Kindle Book.

[20] Myer Pearlman. *Knowing the Doctrines of the Bible* (Springfield, MO: Gospel Publishing House, 1937), 219.

because we could not do it for ourselves. Quite often we hear the term "as if I'd never sinned" in relation to justification. Although it isn't the perfect analogy, it is fairly close. It means that God now sees us through the blood of His Son Jesus, as if we had never sinned. Jesus was the sacrifice that made this possible. Without that sacrifice there would be no redemption, and humankind would be forever lost in sin. Hebrews 9:22 (NKJV) tells us that "without the shedding of blood there is no remission." It is through this blood of Jesus that we can now be restored to fellowship with the Father. It's not just that our sins have been forgiven (they have) but that they have been removed, obliterated, and are gone, just as if we had never sinned. Hence the term.

Conversion and Regeneration

Conversion quite simply is the opposite side of repentance (just like two sides of the same coin) and happens at the same instant as repentance. Whereas repentance is turning away from something (our sinful life), conversion is our turning toward God.[21] When we repent we turn away from sin, and in the turning away we turn toward God. Repentance and conversion are things humankind does for salvation, and they are the only things.

There is a distinction between conversion and regeneration, according to Shedd:

> Regeneration is an act; conversion is an activity or a process. Regeneration is the origination of life; conversion is the evolution and manifestation of life. Regeneration is wholly an act of God; conversion is wholly an activity of man. Regeneration is a

---

[21]   Wayne Grudem, *Bible Doctrine: Essential Teachings of the Christian Faith* (Grand Rapids, MI: Zondervan, 1999), 311.

cause; conversion is an effect. Regeneration is instantaneous; conversion is continuous.[22]

At this point the Holy Spirit comes to live inside of us and brings life (regeneration). That same grace that so graciously saves us also sets us free. When the scripture says the truth shall set you free, that is itself truth. Scripture clearly tells us that Jesus is the way, the truth, and the life; no one comes to the father except through Him (Jn 14:6 NIV). Nor is there any other name under heaven through which humans can be saved (Acts 4:12).

This great work that God began in us has been His plan all along. It originated in Him, and He alone brings it to fruition. It is His transcendent grace working in us that brings us to the point of conviction of our sin and then so graciously forgives us and leads us through the experience to a whole new life in Christ.[23]

James said every good and perfect gift comes from above (Jas 1:16–18). It is divine grace; it comes from above; it is salvific; it is eternal. It is that momentary transaction of faith that occurs when our sins are forgiven, and we are literally delivered from the power of darkness to the kingdom of His Son (Col 1:13).

As great and glorious as this salvation is, it is only the beginning. He promised never to leave us or forsake us (Heb 13:5). The Holy Spirit now dwells within us, and He gives us the victory over the bondage from which we have been freed.

He gives us power to say no to those things that had bound us. He gives us wisdom to say yes to those things that are pleasing to Him. He teaches us God's word and brings us to an obedient loving relationship with our Father.

This is a complete and total new life in Him. Regeneration is the beginning of a radical reversal in moral character away from the

---

[22]   G. T. Shedd. *Dogmatic Theology*, third ed. (Phillipsburg, NJ: P and R Publishing, 2003), 763.

[23]   Herman Bavinck. *Reformed Dogmatics* (Grand Rapids, MI: Baker Academic, 2011), 476.

inordinate love of creaturely goods to the rewards of walking in the way of holiness (Calvin, Inst 2.3.6).[24] Calvin speaking on Psalm 100:3 points out that that "regeneration, is the commencement of the spiritual life."[25]

Our sins have been forgiven—past, present, and even future. We have the assurance of the Holy Spirit that we are indeed saved. Now this grace is not a "cheap grace," and it certainly does not give us a free pass to sin—quite the contrary. It was bought for us at the greatest of price, which is the blood of our Lord Jesus Christ on Calvary. In Romans 6:14, Paul states, "For sin shall no longer have dominion over you, because you are no longer under the law." Simply stated we are new creations, no longer under the bondage of sin. The Scottish preacher George McDonald wrote, "The notion that the salvation of Jesus is a salvation from punishment for our sins is a mean, selfish, low notion. He was called Savior because he would save us from our sins."[26]

We as Christians are not perfect; we are more like newborn babies. Hence the common phrase of being "born again." We are just there, all newly born, washed and clean and full of potential. We are ready to begin life all over again. God in His great mercy, grace, and love gave us an opportunity for a "do over." No matter how vile the sin, He offers forgiveness and new life. Regardless of the enormity of that sin or the quantity of sins, Freil tells us that "no one can out sin God's grace."[27] His grace is more than sufficient to remove anyone's sin. Saul of Tarsus was a prime example. He himself said he was the "worst" of sinners, and God's grace eradicated his sin (1 Tm 1:15 NIV).

---

[24] Oden, 617.

[25] John Calvin, *Institutes of the Christian Religion* (Bellingham, WA: Logos Bible Software, 1997).

[26] Peter Kreeft and Ronald K. Tacelli, *Handbook of Christian Apologetics* (Downers Grove, IL: Intervarsity Press, 1994), 321.

[27] Todd Freil, *Wretched TV* (NRB Broadcasting).

So often, people see salvation as the end. A person has said the prayer, accepted or made a decision for Christ, and that's it. A person's sins are forgiven, and that person is now headed for heaven, no matter what is done from that time forward. But is this the end of the story? Oddly enough, it is just the beginning.

In Ephesians 2:4–10, Paul states that Christ has made us alive together with Him, whereas before this we were dead in our trespasses and sin. Notice the word *together*, which is in the present tense. It means that we are being saved. The Bible speaks of salvation in three tenses: past, present, and future. "For we are unto God a sweet savor of Christ, in they that are being saved (present tense), and to them who are perishing" (2 Cor 2:15). Now, back to Ephesians 2:5–8: "Even when we were dead in sins, He hath quickened us together with Christ; it is by grace you have been saved." *Saved*, here, is in the past tense. In verse 8, again in the past tense, it says, "For it is by grace you have been saved through faith; and that not of yourselves: it is the gift of God." In 2 Timothy 1:9 (NIV), Paul writes: "He has saved us and called us to a holy life—not because of anything we have done but because of His own purpose and grace. This grace was given us in Christ Jesus before the beginning of time." Then, in Matthew 10:28 (NIV), Jesus says, "You will be hated by everyone because of me, but the one who stands firm to the end will be saved." Here salvation is in future tense.

So we can honestly say that we "have been" saved, that we "are (in the process of) being" saved, and that "we will be saved," and be correct. It is instantaneous and also progressive throughout our lives. Yet even so, it is God's work of grace in us. It is not something we do to merit it.

We are saved by grace alone and not by anything we could earn on our own, regardless of how "good" we may think we are or how hard we try. It is God's plan from beginning to end. We simply acknowledge coming to God in repentance and asking forgiveness and placing our trust or faith in Him to save us.

Here is where we ask the question of what happens next. Do we continue living the same life as we did before coming to Christ? Is that the extent of grace? If so, it would still be grace beyond all of our wildest understanding and imaginings. Or does grace actually continue to work throughout our lives?

Conclusion

Well, we know that Christ gives us the Holy Spirit and that He now indwells our hearts, where grace is extended to every believer through Him, working in our lives. He came to take up residence at the time of our salvation. At the same time the Holy Spirit creates within us a hunger to learn more about Jesus and gives us a desire to learn what the Bible says. There is no Christianity apart from the Bible. It is God's written word to us. The Holy Spirit is part of the godhead and therefore Himself God. He knows the word of God because He wrote it. He is the one who begins to open our eyes and helps us to see all throughout the scriptures all that God has done and has in store for us. This is so we can know how to please Him and walk in His ways. Scripture shows us that God has plans for each of us, and they are plans to prosper us, not harm us (Jer 29:11 NIV).

This process is called sanctification, and it is instantaneous in the moment of our new birth at conversion. It is progressive in that it is a lifelong commitment to make us holy. It is this sanctification that we will deal with in more detail later.

There are so many aspects to salvation, just as a diamond has many facets, but still only one diamond. So it is with salvation. It envelopes so many areas. Nelson writes that in the Hebrew and Greek, "salvation implies deliverance, safety, preservation, healing and soundness." Whereas in the gospel it is more of a conglomerate encompassing all "redemptive acts. Justification, redemption, grace, propitiation, imputation, forgiveness, sanctification and glorification."[28]

Our salvation is so wide and so diverse, and we will do well never to forget it. It is the foundation upon which we as Christians can build. Without the sure foundation of our salvation we are building upon the shifting sand. It is the beginning of our Christian walk and the underlying foundation upon which all else is built. We must be sure our foundation is secure. Everything else depends upon it. It is the pillar of our lives as Christians. It holds us up and keeps us sound. It is similar to the way that a horse's legs uphold the horse. Jesus Christ is our sure foundation.

---

[28] P. C. Nelson, *Bible Doctrines* (Springfield, MO: Gospel Publishing House, 1948), 47.

2
CHAPTER

Holiness of God

Where exactly does one start with a subject as complex as holiness? Is there a way that any one person or group of persons could fully comprehend the holiness of God? John Fletcher says, "As we cannot grasp the Universe with our hands, so we cannot comprehend the Maker of the Universe with our thoughts."[29] So we begin this study with humble hearts. Knowing that, we proceed with much fear and trembling.[30] Who can truly know the depths of God's holiness, except God Himself?

The question arises that if we are saved by grace, then why is the subject of holiness important? Good question. The answer to that is that we as Christians need to understand God's holiness. This is so we can offer a proper response to that knowledge.

There is only one sure place to find the answers we seek. That is within the pages of the Bible.

---

[29] John Fletcher, *The Works of John Fletcher* (Schmul Reprints, 1974), vol. 2, 402–403.

[30] John Charles Ryle, *Holiness:Its Nature, Hindrances, Difficulties And Roots* (Lightbydesign.net: Kindle Books).

The Bible

The Bible is undoubtedly the most controversial book in the world. Within its pages there is life. It is there we find the power to have our lives transformed. There we find the answers to our lifelong questions such as what we are and why we are here. It is not the book itself that does this. Nonetheless, as we read it and come to the saving knowledge of Christ, it transforms us (Rom 12:1–2). The Bible tells us about Jesus and how He died for our sin and rose again on the third day. We also learn from the Bible that one day we who have placed our faith in Jesus to save us will be raised together with Him for eternity. It is not a magical book or a textbook. Yet, it is far from being any ordinary book. Cho would have this to say about the Bible: "It is far more than a book because it, like creation itself is the word of God (Ps 138:2)."[31]

The Bible is the book of humankind's redemption. It is the story of our liberation from death, sin, and its entanglement (1 Cor 1:30 NLT). At the same time, it is not just telling a story. It is God revealing Himself to us,[32] leading us to the restoration of fellowship with God. Without a doubt it is the greatest story ever told, in the past or the present or in time to come.

Craig Blomberg says that "church history points out that godly men have used many lofty words to describe the scriptures: words like inspired, God-given, God-breathed, infallible, indefectible, wholly reliable, trustworthy, true, unchanging, and all without any mixture of error. All the while stressing that it is not just to be believed; it is also to be obeyed."[33]

---

[31] Dr. Paul Yonggi Cho, *The Fourth Dimension* (Plainsfield, NJ.: Logos, Int), 40.

[32] Francis Schaeffer, *He Is There and He Is Not Silent* (London: Hodder and Stroughton, 1972), 80.

[33] Graig L. Blomberg, *Can We Still Believe the Bible?* (Grand Rapids, MI: Brazos Press, 2014), 81.

As a Christian our final assessment of the Word of God is that everything should be measured in comparison to it. It is the absolute truth with which we judge all things. It is through the scriptures that God has chosen to reveal Himself and His character. As Kevin DeYoung says, "God's word is the self-disclosure of God to us. It is His word that makes Christ the Word of God incarnate, available, real, and knowable to us (Mt 10:14–15, Jn 15:4–8, Ex 19:5). God is nearest to His people when His people are in His word (Dt 4:7–8, 30:11–14). When God's word is present in us, the Holy Spirit is near (Ps 33:6; Is 34:16, 59:21; Jn 6:63). God's speech has divine attributes (Ps 19:119). Not to mention that the Word itself does things only God is capable of doing (Heb 4:12–13)."[34]

The Bible has always been held in high esteem among believers down through the ages. Those times when it was not, the church suffered. As Christians we do not worship the Bible; we just hold it in high esteem. Listen to John Frame on the subject. He claims "the psalmist revered the words of God with religious awe, as if they had encounters with God Himself. Considering that idolatry was such a serious offense, this was quite odd. Scripture constantly warns about worshipping anything other than God. However, when Christians praise God's word is not idolatry, for to praise God's word is to praise God Himself."[35]

Although we look to many other books and writings in order to get a better understanding of the Bible, it is the Bible itself to which we always defer, bringing all things in subjection to it. So if we want a better understanding of God's Holiness we turn to the Bible as our main source.

---

[34] Kevin DeYoung, http://www.equip.org/Christian-research-journal/volume 35, number 02, (2012).

[35] John M. Frame, *The Doctrine of the Word of God* (Phillipsburg, NJ: P & R Publishing, 2010), 64.

Who God Is

It is through the Bible that we learn we will never comprehend everything about who God is. The Bible doesn't tell us. It merely presupposes that God is. Nor does it try to convince us of the reality of God. God simply is (Gn 1:1). When revealing Himself to Moses in the burning bush, when asked who He was He replied, "I Am that I Am" (Ex 3:14). He just is—always was and always will be. Therefore we just accept the fact that He is.

J. I. Packer says: "The bible does not demand belief in a god: it commands belief in The God." [36] As we begin to search the Bible for answers, God begins to reveal His character to us. Without a doubt the greatest revelation of God to humans was Jesus—who was according to Colossians 1:18 the very image of the invisible God. It says that in Jesus the fullness of the godhead dwelt. Much of what God revealed about Himself comes from the Old Testament, particularly Psalm 19 where the psalmist points to God's creation. In the New Testament, Jesus backed up these claims of God by His life, ministry, and the miracles He performed.

Character and Attributes

It is imperative that we have an accurate knowledge of who God is. Dr. Walter Martin, among many other scholars and theologians, agrees that two main factors inevitably lead people astray. Those are: (1) a misunderstanding of the character of God, and (2) a misunderstanding of the deity of Christ. Most cults and heresy within the church arise from one or the other of these two misconceptions and quite possibly from both.[37]

---

[36] J.I. Packer, *Knowing God* (Downers Grove, IL: Inter-Varsity Press, 1973), 48.

[37] Dr. Walter Martin, *Kingdom of the Cults* (Minneapolis, Minn: Bethany Fellowship, Inc, Publishers, 1977).

So we want to be sure to get a proper understanding of the true nature of God. If we get everything else correct and miss these points, then we have misplaced our faith.[38]

W. A. Pratney said: "Because God is the ultimate reality, we must measure everything against the criterion of His self-revelation and work from what He says outward. Not attempting to make Him fit our personal images and imaginations."[39]

His nature consists of His omnipotence (being all powerful), omniscience (all knowing), and omnipresence (can be everywhere at once). He is eternal. He is immortal. He is Invisible. He is sovereign. As Pratney said: "There is no other like Him. He rules with absolute authority as only our creator has the right to do. He controls everything."[40]

He is immutable Wayne Grudem has this to say: "He does not change. He hasn't changed His mind" (Ps 102:25–27). It is because of this unchanging quality that God is infinitely worthy of trust because He is absolutely and eternally unchanging in His being, perfections, purposes, and promises.[41]

Therefore if the Bible establishes that God was holy in the beginning it is safe to say that He is still holy today and will continue to be (Heb 13:8).

He is self-sufficient (in need of nothing or no one). He is uncreated (meaning He is not created by anyone or anything else and is Himself the creator of heaven and earth). He is transcendent, being above all that He has created and separate from. He is also holy, just, and righteous. God is all of these things and so much more.

---

[38] W. A. Pratney, *The Nature And Character of God.* (Minneapolis, MN: Bethany House Publishing, 1988), 90.

[39] Ibid., 92.

[40] Warren W. Wiersbe, *Be Holy, "Be" Commentary Series* (Wheaton, IL: Victor Books, 1996), 17. Logos.

[41] Wayne Grudem, *Bible Doctrine: Essential Teachings of the Christian Faith* (Grand Rapids, MI: Zondervan, 1999),73–74.

We should remember that none of these attributes should be taken and exalted above any others. For instance, we cannot separate the love of God from the rest of His attributes. No one attribute is superior to the others. Tim Conway would explain it like this: When we consider that "God is His attributes," being all of these things and more, we should be careful not to separate or elevate any one above the others. To elevate one at the expense of the others would produce a separate or segmented god. When we do this we may find ourselves not serving the God of the Bible but a God of our own making.[42] When we emphasize a God of love, or holiness, or grace and overlook all of His other attributes as being equal, we have a distorted view of God. He is all of these things and so much more.

It is easy to be swayed by the notion that God is love, and He most certainly is. What we need to understand is that while God is a God of love, He is also the God of justice and wrath. Although John 4:8 tells us that God is love, this does not mean that this is the total essence of His being. His love is merely one of His core attributes. Some would argue that even God's wrath is an aspect of His love.[43]

We must be careful to not divide any of His attributes. It is interesting that Wiesbe says, "Love without holiness would be a monstrous thing that could destroy God's perfect law, while holiness without love would leave no hope for the lost sinner. They are perfectly balanced in the divine nature and works of God."[44] They are two wings on the same bird that grant the bird the ability to fly straight and true.

---

[42] Tim Conway, *Holiness of God*, http://illbehonest.com/Holiness-of-God-Tim-Conway.

[43] Peter Kreeft & Ronald K Tacelli, *Handbook of Christian Apologetics* (Downers Grove, IL: InterVarsity Press, 1994), 289.

[44] Warren W. Wiersbe, 184.

God's Holiness

Since the topic of this writing is holiness, we should concentrate on how it differs from the rest of God's attributes.

Author Ray Dunning put it this way: "First we must take into account of the way the holiness of God informs to attempt to ascribe attributes to God. There are three theories that have been offered by theologians."

1. Holiness is one attribute among others.
2. Holiness is the sum total of all the attributes.
3. Holiness is the backbone for all the attributes.

When looking over the list we can see that:

1. Holiness is not just one attribute among others. God's holiness permeates every aspect of His character.
2. We can rule out number two because holiness is not the sum total of all the other attributes. Rather, one should be inclined to think that all of the other attributes are contingent upon holiness.
3. So we are left with number three. This is the reality, as holiness is the backbone for all other attributes.[45]

R. C. Sproul explains this when he tells us that holiness is like an umbrella encompassing all the others. As a result, God's love is holy. His wrath is holy. His justice is holy. Every attribute of God is holy. So we can see that every other attribute of God is enhanced or modified by holiness. He goes on to say that "God's holiness isn't simply the absence of defilement, a negative thing. The holiness

---

[45]   Ray H. Dunning, *Grace, Faith & Holiness* (Kansas City, MO: Beacon Hill Press, 1988), 192.

of God is positive and active. It's God's perfect nature at work in accomplishing God's perfect will."[46]

Bavnick would point out that if we look to the past we will see that pagan religions did not have, nor do they now have, any concept of the holiness of God. They simply didn't know anything of sin or grace.[47] This is still true today. Only the God of the Bible is holy and righteous. Robert Diffinbaugh would comment that "one who is holy is uniquely holy, with no rivals or competition." From this statement we can see that. Jehovah, the God of the Bible, was the only God known for His holiness; this is what set Him apart from all the other gods throughout history—this one distinguishing feature, holiness (Ex 15:11).[48]

It is clear that God's nature is loving, gracious, merciful, holy, and just. But what else does the Bible say? One of the most incredible verses is John 3:16, which many of us learned by memory in Sunday school when we were children. It is probably the most famous Bible verse of all time. We have preached it, memorized it, sung it, and applied it to just about every circumstance and surface known to humans. However, does anyone really look beyond the obvious and ask why? We speak of God's great love, and we should. It is great and unfathomable. But do we ever stop to ponder why the sacrifice was required in the first place? A sacrifice was required because God is holy. As great as His love was for humankind, there could be no fellowship between the two until sin was atoned for. John 3:16 speaks loudly of the holiness of God.

Jay Kesler stresses the point that in the Bible the place where the holiness of God is most powerfully portrayed is at Calvary. Why? Because God is "so holy, so utterly holy," that nothing short of Christ's death could make amends. Only then could He forgive

---

[46] R. C. Sproul, *Holiness of God.*

[47] Herman Bavinck, *Reformed Dogmatics* (Grand Rapids, MI: Baker Academic, 2011).

[48] Robert L. Diffenbaugh, *God's Holiness.* http://bible.org/servespage/5-holiness-god.

us. He would go on to say, "The cross is the supreme and sublime declaration of the holiness of God." At the cross God's holiness and justice were appeased. It was because He loved us and there was no other way God's holiness and justice could be resolved other than the cross. The cross was necessary because of His holiness.[49]

As such the barrier of sin that stood between sinful humankind and a holy God needed to be removed. Sin was and still is a very serious issue. The only thing that has changed is that now God has made provision for our sin through His Son.

Sin

Sin is a blight on the human race. In order to get a firm understanding of the holiness of God we need to understand how grievous sin is to God.

Because God is holy, we know that He cannot even look upon sin. Jesus was sinless and holy and walked in perfect obedience in His life here on earth, yet God could not look upon Him at His crucifixion. Not because of any sin He had committed. Rather it was our sin that He bore on the cross that caused God to look away. Kesler agrees when he says that one of the manifestations of God's holiness is His abhorrence of sin and His separation from sin, sinners, and all evil. Even the Old Testament was God's revelation of the holiness of God and how God responded to it. The law itself was to reveal to Israel and to the world around them the holiness of God. The tabernacle was designed to represent God's holiness along with the ceremonial law and teaching on clean and unclean animals. All of this was to represent the concept of His holiness and that they

---

[49]   Jay Kesler, *Being Holy, Being Human: Dealing with the Expectations of Ministry,* Leadership Library, Vol. 13. (Carol Stream, IL: Waco, TX: *Christianity Today Inc.*: Word Books, 1988) vol 13, 17, 18. Logos.

(the Israelites) were to be a people set apart from the rest of the world by walking in holiness.[50]

God is holy; therefore sin is repulsive to Him. Think about that for a bit. If sin is repulsive to God, then why are we Christians so willing to accept it in our lives and the lives of others? It would seem that sometimes sinners, not we Christians, seem to realize the seriousness of sin to a holy God more than we do. It is because God is holy that "His eyes are too pure to (look upon) evil, and thou cannot look on wickedness with favor" (Hab 1:13, Ps 5:4–6). The only way for God to remove sin was by the death of a substitute sacrifice. No other sacrifice than the death of Christ could have removed our sin. As a result of God's moral character, He hates sin and is provoked to consume it in judgment.[51]

Watson writes that we can perceive the vileness of sin simply by the price required of it. There was no remedy for sin except the blood of Jesus. Only God's blood could atone for sin. No king or prince on earth, according to Augustine, or angel in heaven could remove the curse of sin. Only the blood of Jesus that was shed on the cross at Calvary was capable of that atonement. We might think the curse of sin was that every human was affected by it. In reality it was because Christ had to die for it.[52]

Simply to dismiss the death sentence for sin was impossible, for "He cannot deny Himself" (2 Tm 2:13). Therefore God's consuming hatred of sin necessitates a salvation in which the execution of His hatred of sin is completely carried out in the full punishment of sin.[53]

Even in our simplest and most beloved of salvation verses, God's holiness is addressed. That is what the cross of Calvary was about. It is about the holiness of God and His hatred of sin. God cannot be separated from His holiness. Why? Because He is holy. His holiness

---

[50]   Kesler, 17.

[51]   Robert A. Morey. *Studies in the Atonement.* (Orange, CA:Christian Scholars Press, 2007)

[52]   Thomas Watson. *A body of Divinity* (googgle books), 147

[53]   Morey.

is an awesome and fearful thing—awesome to those who belong to Him through faith in Christ. We stand in awe and wonder at His great love, grace, and mercy that was extended to us. But that is fearful, to those who reject that same offer of love, grace, and mercy.

We hear so much today about "being in the presence of God." This usually pertains to dancing and singing and all sorts of ecstatic behavior. But one has to ask himself or herself this: How did the saints of old react in the presence of God? More often than not they threw themselves face down before Him in fear and trembling. Great revivals of the past were accompanied by weeping and repentance as people realized their sinful condition before a holy God.[54] The Bible says it is a fearful thing to fall into the hands of the living God (Heb 10:31). When we truly come into the presence of God we should be humbled as our sin becomes radically visible to us. Why? Because God's holiness is so real that we cannot stand in His Holy presence in our sinful state. Our only hope is to have our sins forgiven and placed under the precious blood of Jesus Christ.

When in Isaiah 6, Isaiah is before God's throne the first thing to strike Him was His sin. He was a man of unclean lips. So it is when we enter into the presence of God. It is with reverence and awe as we are humbled by our sin before a Holy God.

It is interesting that in Isaiah's description of the throne room he points to the seraphim on either side of the mercy seat! In the presence of God they cry out to one another, "Holy, holy, holy." Makes one wonder why they didn't shout out "Love, love, love" or "Grace, grace, grace." We see the same thing in Revelation 4:6–8, where John sees four living creatures before the throne crying out, "Holy, holy, holy." Why not, "Mercy, mercy, mercy?" This is because holiness is the one character trait that encompasses all of the others. God is holy and every aspect of Him is holy. R. C. Sproul says, "Holiness is the only attribute raised to the 3rd degree or the only

---

54   Andrew Strom, *True and False Revival* (Revival School Publishers, 2008), 44.

one characteristic of God that is carried to the third level. This is a dimension of God that consumes His very essence."[55]

Hopefully, when we see or quote John 3:16 we will see the scope of all that it embraces, so that we may understand the holiness of God and what a serious subject it is for Christians. Not just the love of God but also His holiness breaking forth.

Conclusion

For many today, happiness not holiness is the main pursuit. They want Jesus to solve their problems and carry their burdens. Yet they don't want Him to control their lives or change their character. However eight times in the Bible, God said to His people, "Be holy, for I am holy." This was never meant to be multiple choice. Jonathan Edwards wrote this: "He that sees the beauty of holiness, or true moral good, sees the greatest and most important thing in the world." Wiersbe would back this up by noting, "The emphasis of the Bible is on the holiness of God and not on the love of God." "Love is central in God," wrote American theologian Augustus H. Strong, "but holiness is central in love. God's love is a holy love."[56]

When we acknowledge that God is holy, we come into agreement with who God says He is and what the Bible reveals about Him.

The word *holy* is used ninety-one times in Leviticus. Words connected with cleansing are used seventy-one times. References to uncleanness number 128. The book of Leviticus itself is quoted or referred to over one hundred times in the New Testament. According to 2 Timothy 3:16, all scripture is given by God and is profitable to us. The book of Leviticus is about the law and holiness. Jesus

---

[55] R. C. Sproul, *The Importance of Holiness*, www.ligonier.org/learn/series/holiness_of_God/the_importance-of-holiness/?

[56] Warren W. Wiersbe, *Be Holy*, "Be" Commentary Series (Wheaton, IL: Victor Books, 1996), 17.

Himself said that we are to live by every word that proceeds from the word of God (Mt 4:4). God's Word extols the holiness of God.[57]

Exodus 15:11 says, "Who is like Thee among the gods, O LORD? Who is like Thee, majestic in holiness? Awesome in praises, working wonders?"

> There is no one holy like the LORD. Indeed there is no one besides Thee, Nor is there any rock like our God. (1 Sam 2:2)

> There is no one like Thee among the gods O Lord. Nor are there any works like thine. All the nations whom Thou hast made shall come and worship before thee, O Lord: And they shall glorify thy name. For Thou art great and do wondrous deeds. Thou alone art God. (Ps 86:8–10)

> All declare the Holiness of God. (Ps 99:1–3; Is 40:25, 57:15)

> God Himself is called the Most Holy One. (Ps 71:22, 78:41, 89:18; Is 1:4–5, 5:19, 24, 6:3; Ps 99:9, 99:3–5, 22:3)

Herman Bavink said: "God is called the 'Holy One of Israel.' This is one of the repeated names of Jehovah in Scripture. It is used 30 times in Isaiah, alone."[58]

---

[57] Ibid. Weirsbe,10.
[58] Herman Bavink, *Reformed Dogmatics* (Grand Rapids, MI: Baker Academic).

Nor is Holiness primarily a moral attribute. Rather it refers to that absolute "otherness" that distinguishes the divine from all that is creaturely, and so characterizes every aspect of God.[59]

Because God is holy, He also commands His followers to be holy as He is. To know the holiness of God is to change our perspective in how we relate to Him. He is our creator who made us in His image. If we are made in the image of God then we should be holy, which is what His word states. This is the subject we are going to deal with in the upcoming chapters.

Holiness is the moral excellence of God that unifies His attributes and is expressed through His actions, setting Him apart from all others. Believers are called to be holy as God is holy.[60]

We can safely ascertain from this that God is indeed holy, though we understand that one attribute cannot be elevated above the others, as they all together make up the character of God. We have singled out the attribute of holiness to acquire a clearer understanding of it.

Manser put it this way: "This holiness is the quality of God that sets him utterly apart from his world, especially in terms of his purity and sanctity."[61] It is also not wrong to say that holiness does, for lack of a better word, seem to be the glue that adheres all the attributes together.

It is important to examine God's holiness since He is holy. This is so that we as His children can live our lives in accordance with that holiness, but not for our salvation because that has been established through faith in Christ. On the contrary it is due to the fact that we are so thankful for all He has done for us. Now the

---

[59]   Langdon B. Gilkne, *Maker of Heaven and Earth* (Garden City, NY: Double Day, 1959), 89.

[60]   Warren W. Wiersbe, 17.

[61]   Martin H. Manser, *Dictionary of Bible Themes: The Accessible and Comprehensive Tool for Topical Studies* (London: Martin Manser, 2009), Logos.

great desire of our hearts is to serve and love Him in a manner that is pleasing to Him. We have established the holiness of God and are now ready to begin a study to see why holiness is needed in the life of the believer.

3

CHAPTER

The Need for Holiness

If ever there was a need for holiness it is now—in our lives, our homes, our churches, our communities, and our nation. No message has been so neglected or misunderstood in the church as that of holiness for the believer. We have seen the speaking in tongues, the gifts of the Spirit being manifested, demons put to flight, people healed, and miracles in our midst. Even so, we are perceived as hypocrites by those outside the church. How is this possible? Is this the same church that the Bible describes Jesus coming for? One that is spotless, pure, and faultless without blemish? (Eph 5:27)[62] Or as Michael Brown put it, "Our nation is infected with moral rot because the Church has failed to be the Light, to shine the Light, or to walk in the Light."[63]

As a result, Christians are no longer seen as being honest in their dealing or upright in their behavior. It is one of the things that has

[62] William T. Shedd, *Dogmatic Theology*, 3rd ed. (Phillipsburg, NJ: Presbyterian and Reformed Publishing, 2003), 805.
[63] Michael L. Brown, *Go and Sin No More: A Call to Holiness* (Regal Books:ISBN:978-0-615-73019-6, 1999), 15.

led to the church being held up to such ridicule today. There is a lack of integrity and morals in the church. This would seem normal if we were describing the world and the unsaved. Yet these are the accusations being made against the church.

Where is that transforming power of the Holy Spirit in the lives of Christians that Paul speaks of in Romans 12:1–2? What has become of that line of demarcation that separates the holy from the unholy? Has it been completely lost as it was in the days before the flood of Noah?[64] Has it become so hazy that we can no longer distinguish the difference between good and evil? Even Christians are so caught up in sin that some entire churches cannot see the truth from error. Has God not called His church to be separate and set apart from the world?

Dr. Michael Brown puts it very clearly when he states that one of the largest problems we face in the church today is a total disregard for obedience while freely excusing our sin. Stating that we live like God intends for us to "scorn the commandments and disregard His standards as if disobedience were the new norm." Didn't Jesus say that the one who sins is a slave to sin? (Jn 8:34–36). It is apparent that holiness is not an option or multiple choice for a Christian. Anything other than holiness is disobedience.[65]

The good news is that before we were saved we were lost and dead in our trespasses and sin. Now we have been raised to new life in Him (Eph 2:1–6).

So, what is it about our need for holiness that is so disturbing? Is it the recognition that even Christians will one day stand before a holy God to give an account for their actions in this life?[66]

John Bevere says this:

---

[64]   Alfred M. Rehwinkel, *The Flood: In Light of Geology and Archaeology* (St. Louis, MO: Concordia Publishing, 1951).

[65]   Michael L. Brown, *Go and Sin No More: A Call To Holiness* (Regal Books, 1999), 95.

[66]   Mark A. Quanstrom, *From Grace to Grace* (Kansas City, MO: Beacon Hill Press, 2011), 20–21.

There is a Judgment Day, which has been appointed from the foundation of the world (Acts 17:3). That day will not bring new revelation of truth; rather, it will measure all things what has already been spoken. God's Word which we currently possess, will judge us in that last day. It is eternal. It is final. There are no exceptions, alterations, or revisions. Wouldn't it benefit us to know and live by what He says, rather than make assumptions about what He said? That judgment will be based on how we aligned our lives with God's eternal word.[67]

Paul's statement in 2 Corinthians 5:10 (NLT) says, "For we must all stand before Christ to be judged. We will each receive whatever we deserve for the good or evil we have done in this earthly body. We may not face the same judgment as the unbelievers, but we will be called to give an accurate account of how we managed this life.

When we recognize that God is holy and understand that heaven is going to be a holy place, devoid of sin, we begin to appreciate what manner of life we as His children should be living here on earth. Nancy Pearcey mentions, "Most churches although strong on teaching conversion, they are very weak on teaching about how to live after conversion."[68] So we must ask ourselves, how exactly are Christians supposed to live after coming to Christ?

Craig Bloomberg spells it out nicely with: "The pathway into a deeper experience of God's love is the pathway of holiness."[69] Although our salvation is secured in Christ through repentance and

[67] John Bevere. *Driven by Eternity: Make Your Life Count Today and Forever* (Palmer Lake, CO: Messenger International, 2016), 12.

[68] Nancy Pearcey, *Total Truth: Liberating Christianity from Its Cultural Captivity* (Wheaton, IL: Crossway Books, 2005), 49.

[69] Craig L. Bloomberg, *Can We Still Believe the Bible? An Evangelical Engagement With Contemporary Questions* (Grand Rapids, MI: Brazos Press, 2007), 88.

faith, this repentance that precedes faith signifies not only a turning away from something but also a turning toward something. Is there something else required of us once we are saved? If so, what is it? While our salvation is God's free gift to us, might discipleship cost us something? All of Christ's disciples would agree that their salvation was by grace alone. Yet, to follow Jesus it cost them everything including their lives. So do we as Christians have a responsibility in regard to that gift that was so graciously given? Many would say no. But what does the Bible say?

If a person were to hand the keys of a new car to another person, thereby giving it to him or her, would the recipient of that new vehicle not be expected to appreciate and maintain and care for that car? What if the person neglected it, wrecked it, or turned around and gave it to someone else? How would that make the one giving that gift feel? Would that vehicle not require care and maintenance to keep it in good running shape? Oil changes, fuel, tires, etc. Would one not cherish it? Therefore is it unfair to think that God expects us to cherish our precious, priceless gift of salvation? The gift beyond price.

Nelson states: "The Scriptures teach a life of holiness without which no man shall see the Lord. By the power of the Holy Ghost we are able to obey the command, 'Be ye holy, for I am holy.' Sanctification is the will of God for all believers, and should be earnestly pursued by walking in obedience to God's Word" (Heb 12:14, 1 Pt 1 15–16, 1 Thes 5:23–24, 1 Jn 2:6).[70]

Let's take a quick look at Ephesians 2:8–10 for a moment where it says,

> For by grace you have been saved through faith,
> and that not of yourselves; *it is* the gift of God,
> not of works, lest anyone should boast. For we are

---

[70] P. C. Nelson, *Bible Doctrines* (Springfield, MO: Gospel Publishing House, 1948), 102.

His workmanship, created in Christ Jesus for good
works, which God prepared beforehand that we
should walk in them.

Well, first we notice that we are saved by grace—nothing we
merited or did ourselves. It is a gift. Notice though that it goes on to
say in verse 10 that we are His workmanship created *for* good works,
which God prepared beforehand that we should *walk* in them.

So we were not just saved, as in to have fire insurance to keep us
from the fires of hell, as some would claim. But for a bigger purpose.
Therefore we do the works not to be saved; we work because we are
saved. We were saved for a purpose—that purpose being good works
that God Himself created for each of us.

James 2:13–20 says, "Show me your faith without works, and
I will show you my faith by my works." What James is saying here
is that we really can't show our faith without works. Our works are
evidence of our faith. Let us love not in word only. John says in 1
John 3:18: "My little children, let us not love in word or in tongue,
but in deed and in truth." The two—faith and works—go hand in
hand.

Our salvation comes from God, not us, although we at some
point have to decide to accept this salvation. Horton would respond,
"It is His work alone that brings us to salvation. The cross itself is
the key to our personal sanctification."[71] Once we have repented and
accepted Christ as our Savior, we have the responsibility to follow
Him and live our lives according to His standards, not ours. He
endows us with His Holy Spirit to guide us, teach us, and keep us
clean. He provides us with His word so that we may discover how to
live for Him in a manner that is pleasing to Him. He brings us the
fellowship of other believers to help, teach, and encourage us along

---

[71]   Stanley M. Horton, *Five Views of Sanctification: The Pentecostal Perspective*
(Grand Rapids, MI: Zondervan, 1987), 110.

the way. Still, we know that the decisions we make after conversion will have an effect on where we will spend eternity.[72]

Is it possible for Christians to live in a way that is pleasing to God, as opposed to one that might be displeasing? Scripture would show us that we certainly can live in ways that please God (1 Jn 3:22, 2 Cor 5:9, Rom 12:1 AMP). It is called obedience, and it is brought around by a work of the Holy Spirit called sanctification, which in its own right is just as important to the believer as is justification. "Where justification sets us free from the penalty of sin. Sanctification sets us free from the power of sin."[73] God has called His people to holiness—to be called apart and to be separate from the rest of the world.

Meyer Pearlman, an early Assembly of God man, defines sanctification as, "including **separation** from sin and the world and (2) dedication or consecration, to the fellowship and service of God through Christ." He identifies sanctified and holy as synonymous and adds that "while the primary meaning of holy is that of separation unto service, the idea of purification is also involved."[74]

In the book of Exodus, God delivered the people of Israel from the bondage of Egypt. His goal was to set them apart and make a nation of them. We see that they rebelled over and over again. They desired Egypt. We think this to be strange behavior, in that they could have been so miraculously delivered from the bondage of Egypt, having witnessed the miracles God performed on their behalf such as walking through the Red Sea on dry ground while their enemies drowned behind them. They were led by the hand of God day by day for forty years. God supplied all of their needs on a daily basis. This, however, was not enough for them as they continued complaining and trying God's patience. Was this because

---

[72]   John Bevere, *Eternity, 12.*

[73]   David Pawson, *Once Saved, Always Saved?: A Study in Perseverance and Inheritance* (London, Sydney, Aukland: Hodder & Sloughton, 1996), 16.

[74]   Myer Pearlman, *Knowing the Doctrines of the Bible* (Springfield, MO: Gospel Publishing House, 1937), 266.

they lacked something? No, God supplied them with fresh manna every morning; their clothes and shoes never wore out; no one was sick or hurt. So what was so important in Egypt? They missed the onions and leeks of Egypt.

These were God's people, with whom He made a covenant. That generation never entered the Promised Land nor received the inheritance that was theirs. Why is that? It was because of their rebellion and disobedience. Even Moses their leader didn't enter the Promised Land (Nm 20:12). Could it be that the people wanted deliverance not from Egypt but rather deliverance in Egypt?[75]

What does this have to do with Christians today? We are not so different from those early Israelites. Egypt itself is a type (symbol) of sin in the New Testament.[76] Many today want to have their sins forgiven while remaining in them, believing that there is now no condemnation for them (Rom 8:1). Yet, this way of thinking is a travesty against scripture. As surely as God called those early Israelites to holiness, He has called us to holiness. He has delivered us from sin and its power in our lives. But many who call themselves Christians want salvation with no strings attached and no effort on their part to change their behavior.

As Christians we cannot live a dual life with one foot in the kingdom of God and the other in the world. We dare not ride that fence. Decisions need to be made. Sooner or later one will have to decide on which side to dismount.

Christ came to set us free. He freed us from past sin at Calvary, and in so doing He also broke the power of sin over our lives.[77] The New Testament repeatedly affirms that the believers in Christ have

---

75 John Bevere, *A Heart Ablaze* (Nashville, TN: Thomas Nelson, 1999), 81.

76 David Pawson, 33.

77 Thomas C. Oden, *Classis Christianity: A Systematic Theology* (New York: Harper Collins, 1992), 659.

been set free from sin's power (Rom 6:6, 17, 18, 22). The problem is not that people cannot quit sinning but that they won't.[78]

Another writer puts it this way: Many believers are unfamiliar with scriptural teaching on holiness, leading many to think of it as impossible to attain. Or worse, something theological or theoretical and therefore not viable for believers for today. Some are comfortable thinking of holiness as another doctrine to be believed rather than a virtue to be lived daily. He questions if this is not from an unwillingness to meet the demands of holy living.[79]

Some Christians will argue that holiness is not possible for this life. But is that biblical?

Interestingly enough, Calvin and Wesley both agree on this point—that we have been called to holiness. Although Calvin taught that Jesus kept the law for us so that we wouldn't have to in order to earn our salvation, He insisted that believers should keep God's law as proof of their gratitude for the salvation they had received. Calvin also agreed with Wesley that holy living is the goal of salvation: "since it is especially characteristic of His (God's) glory, that he have no fellowship with wickedness and uncleaness."[80]

Why is holiness for the believer important? Acts 1:8 (NIV) says, "But you shall receive power when the Holy Spirit comes upon you; then you will be a witness of Me in Jerusalem, and in all of Judea and Samaria and to the end of the earth." We need the power of the Holy Spirit in our lives to live for Him. We cannot do it on our own.

Notice it says that we shall *be* witnesses to Him in Jerusalem and in the rest of the world. This is significant because it is not just through words that we bear witness but through our lives as well.

---

78 David A. Servant, *The Great Gospel Deception: Exposing the False Promise of Heaven Without Holiness* (Kindle Edition) ISBN: 978-1-939788-90-0 (ePub edition, 1999).

79 Dr. J. Ayodeji, Adwuya, *Transformed by Grace: Paul's View of Holiness in Romans 6–8.* (Eugene, OR: Cascade Books, 2004), 14.

80 Anthony A. Hoekema, *Five Views of Sanctification: Response to Dieter and the Wesleyan Perspective* (Grand Rapids, MI: Zondervan, 1987), 48.

This requires something more than mere speech. It requires action and effort on our part. What is that action? To live a holy life before God and others. We are told in Philippians 2:5 to "let this mind be in you, which was also in Christ Jesus."

Maturity of Christian life is to be found among those believers who have "put off the old man" (Eph 4:22, 24). Christians are urged to cleanse themselves "from all filthiness of the flesh and spirit" (2 Cor 7:1). "Every thought" is to be brought captive "to obedience of Christ" (2 Cor 10:5). We are to "lay aside every weight and the sin which doth so easily beset us" (Heb 12:1).[81] We are also told to "put on" the full armor of God (Eph 6). Put on, Put off, cleanse, brought, lay aside. These are all active terms—something we do. Even with the acknowledgment that the Holy Spirit is the active agent in sanctification,[82] action is still required on our part.

We understand that the Holy Spirit gives us the unction, strength, knowledge, and wisdom to set these thing in motion. He is the one who prompts us, teaches us, and guides us. We, on the other hand, are the ones who have to surrender and obey. Oden had this to say: "True sanctification is from the Holy Spirit not just acts on our part."[83]

Dieter concurs by saying, "The same teacher the Spirit continues His work today, not by bringing new revelation, but new understanding as He illuminates the truth we study."[84]

Another reason why holiness is important today is because a holy life leads to an effective witness. An old saying among Christians is: "Your actions are so loud that I cannot hear what you are saying."[85] We need to live in such a manner that our lives back up what we

---

[81]   Melvin E. Dieter, *Five Views on Sanctification: The Wesleyan Perspective* (Grand Rapids, MI: Zondervan, 1987), 32–33.

[82]   Ibid., 43.

[83]   Thomas C. Oden, 658.

[84]   Melvin Dieter, 122.

[85]   Peter Kreeft and Ronald K. Tacelli, *Handbook of Christian Apologetics* (Downers Grove, IL:Intervarsity Press, 1994).

are saying. When our actions are out of sync with our words, we are compromised, making us appear false and hypocritical. So we can say with certainty that "without holiness our witness for Christ will be superficial and ineffective." J. C. Ryle puts it like this: "Sound protestant and evangelical doctrine is useless if it is not accompanied by a holy life. It is worse than useless: it does positive harm."[86] M. S. Nulls complies by saying we are never going to effectively present the holiness of God (the conviction of righteousness) if "the vessel of our life is sullied by unforgiven sin." We must sanctify our bodies in order to glorify God, to whom we owe everything.[87]

Jesus set us free from the bondage of sin at Calvary. Not just past sins, but future ones as well. We are no longer bound by sin (Rom 6). He has given us the power to live above this through His grace and the power of His Holy Spirit within us. This does not say, nor is there any implication, that we have a free ticket to sin. However, the word does promise that if we do sin (and we will), if we confess this sin to Him, He will be faithful and just to forgive us and cleanse us from all unrighteousness (1 Jn 1:8–9). This is not talking about practicing or living in sin on a daily basis. That would be living in the darkness mentioned in this same scripture. This applies more to when we stumble or fall unexpectedly or wake up to find ourselves in some sin.

Justification is merely taking the first step. Does God expect His children to grow up and mature?[88] Is this not expected? Sanctification of the believer is every bit as important a work in our lives as is justification, merely a different one. "Sanctification in its place and proportion, is quite as important as justification."[89] Sanctification brings to fruition that which began at justification.

---

[86]   J. C. Ryle, *Holiness: Its Nature, Hindrances, Difficulties, and Roots* (Light By Design.net, 1816–1900). Kindle edition, Introduction.

[87]   M.S. Nulls, *The Life of Christ: A Study Guide to the Gospel Record* (Dallas, TX: 3E Ministries, 1999).

[88]   Nancy Pearcy, 48.

[89]   J.C. Ryle, *Holiness*, Introduction (Kindle).

Spurgeon explains: When a child is born, he can do nothing on his own. He is completely dependent on his parents." This is normal. All his little parts are there and functioning normally. Yet he hasn't learned how to use all these newfound abilities that he has been endowed with. By the time he is ten years of age he should be able to walk, talk, feed himself, tie his shoes and have learned quite a lot about his world. He is still somewhat dependant on his parents for his needs, but not in the same sense as when he was an infant. Now, if that same ten year old boy could not walk, talk or feed himself and was completely helpless, as he was at birth, we would conclude something was wrong with him. It is the same way in the Christian world. When we have been justified by faith in Christ we are as new babies in Christ. At birth (justification) we begin the process (sanctification) of growth and development, so it is in our Christian walk. We are expected to grow and mature in Him.[90]

This is accomplished by reading, hearing, and studying His Word, by being in fellowship with other believers, and by being in communication with Him through prayer. Justification is the introduction; sanctification is the process that takes us forward into our Christian experience. It is where we grow and mature and start to produce fruit worthy of the kingdom. This does not happen overnight. Fruit takes time to mature, while we receive our positional sanctification when we receive Christ, putting us in a right standing with God. The practical side of sanctification is progressive from that point of conversion until we meet Jesus face to face in eternity. It is there where our sanctification will be completed, and it will be said that we have acquired complete sanctification.

It should be pointed out that we will stumble and fall. The first chapter of 1 John makes this very plain. It also tells us we are not without hope. We still have a sin nature; we just need to realize that we now have the power over it. So often, Christians do not know this. The difference is that for true Christians when they fall, they

---

[90]   Charles Spurgeon, *Holiness Demanded*, www.//http.puritandownloads.com.

will not stay there. God has put a new desire in their hearts, and that is the yearning for righteousness. David Servant says, "Those who are truly born again hunger and thirst after righteousness" (Mt 5:6).[91]

This is not in word only, but the evidence will be the transformation in our lives and the changes that come with our salvation. Although we may sin, we no longer abide in it. When realization come that we have sinned, then the Christian will confess and forsake it. J. Vernon McGee once said in one of his broadcasts that the sin that is not forsaken is not forgiven. [92] Servant would be quick to point out,[93] "The grace that forgives also transforms. Thus, people who have not been transformed are not forgiven."

It might be pointed out also that "there is no justification that is not followed by sanctification." For this reason scripture says, "Pursue ... the sanctification without which no one will see the Lord" (Heb 12:14).[94]

A. W. Tozer states that every area of our lives should testify to the majesty of God. All of our public services, not just our private prayers, should be filled with God. Our witnessing, singing, preaching, writing, and teaching should center on the person of our "holy, holy Lord and continually extol the greatness of His dignity and power." Everything we do as Christians privately and corporately should bring glory and honor to God.[95]

Meaning that this is not just holiness in appearance but in every aspect of our lives. As Christians we often view holiness in a very negative light—thinking of it more in terms of being deprived of

---

[91] David A. Servant, *The Great Gospel Deception* (ISBN 978-1-939788-91-7: Kindle edition).

[92] J. Vernon Mcgee, *http://www.oneplace.com/ministries/thru-the-bible-with-j-vernon-mcgee/*

[93] Servant.

[94] David A. Servant, (Kindle), chapter 1.

[95] A.W. Tozer, *The Knowledge of the Holy: The Attributes of God* (New York: Harper Collins, 1897–1963), 184.

some distinct pleasure. In reality it should be viewed in a positive light more with the idea of something of great value to be pursued—a rare opportunity not afforded to all.

When God redeemed us the changes began. That has been His purpose for us all along to have the freedom to live a new and better way, different from our old lifestyle dominated by sin to which we were accustomed. God also knew this to be something we could not do ourselves or within ourselves. It would be too difficult to make those changes that needed to be made.

So God in His great mercy and grace gave us a helper—a teacher to live inside of us and to write God's laws upon our hearts. This helper, who Jesus spoke so affectionately of, is the Holy Spirit. Dieter says that in the New Testament the Holy Spirit takes a greater role—working through sanctification and taking precedence over witnessing, evangelism, giving, and every other service a Christian might perform. It is as we become more like Jesus that we will become more effective in bringing glory to God. It is as we are prompted by the Spirit that we are encouraged in these endeavors, because "God wants us to be something, not just do something."[96]

John Owen simplifies quite nicely by pointing out that the gospel in a nutshell is this: "Jesus came to save us from our sin, not in our sins. He goes on to explain that His blood not only cleanses us from sin, but it frees us from sin as well." He emphasizes that "being born again signals a definite break with a lifestyle dominated by sin.[97]

We cannot begin to fathom the depths of God's grace to those who believe in Him. We know He extended that grace to us in offering us salvation. We dare not limit that same grace that will lead us to heaven. This same grace that saves continues to enable us to live for Him on a daily basis. To say that we cannot live for

---

[96]   Melvin Dieter, 120.

[97]   John Owen, *Temptation and Sin* (Lafayette, IN: Sovereign Grace Publishing, 2001), 8.

Him is in essence to deny that He is able to keep us. To use that grace as an excuse to sin is a terrible grievance against the Holy Spirit. Hebrews 6:4–6 tells us that to go back into sin after having come out of it by faith in Christ is to trample underfoot what Christ accomplished on Calvary. If we were to do such a thing, then what possible redemption is left to us?

Conclusion

Is holiness necessary in the life of a Christian? Yes.

When we say that His righteousness was imputed to us, and therefore nothing is required of us from that time forward, are we truly representing what the Bible teaches? "While it is true that our salvation is by grace our sanctification does require some effort on our part."[98]

In 2 Corinthians 5:17 Paul states: "Therefore, if anyone *is* in Christ, *he is* a new creation; old things have passed away; behold, all things have become new." How can we say this is so, if we continue in our sin? If we return to our old life (or never come out of it to begin with) after having received the forgiveness of sin and being washed in the blood of Jesus Christ, then it might behoove us to take a second look to see if we truly repented as opposed to just having had an emotional experience. According to Swindoll, it is "by faith we confess and forsake our sins; by faith we present ourselves to God; by faith we keep our lives Christ centered; and by faith we obey God's word."[99]

Yes, holiness is important in the Christian life. As Hill would so eloquently put it, "The party is coming to a close."[100] Jesus is

---

[98]   Thomas C. Oden, 657.

[99]   Charles R. Swindoll and Roy B. Zuck, *Understand Christian Theology* (Nashville, TN: Thomas Nelson, 2003), 2003.

[100] Steve Hill, *Spiritual Avalanche* (Lake Mary, FL: Charisma Book Group, 2013), 14.

coming back soon; He is coming back for His beloved bride, the church. Not just any bride either. This one is going to be pure, clean, unblemished, spotless, and holy. As such we need to be ready, and we cannot do this without holiness. It is a time like never before to sound the trumpet for holiness within the body of Christ. He is today calling to Himself a holy church (people). Let us wake up and heed the call, before it is too late. We can and we must live a holy life. It is not a request but a command (1 Pt 1:6, Jas 1:4). Oden would explain it like this: "Perseverance" must finish its work so that you may be mature and whole, not lacking anything.[101]

Heaven is a holy place, and no sin will enter there. Hebrews 12:14 says, "Without holiness no man shall see the Lord." We struggle daily with sin here on earth. When we get to heaven, sin will not be allowed. Let us rid ourselves of sin by submitting to God's word and being obedient (Eph 4:22–29), so that when our name is called we will be ready and unashamed.

---

[101] Thomas C. Oden, 668.

4

CHAPTER

Deity of Jesus

In chapter 2 we talked about there being two main issues concerning a proper understanding of scripture. One of those misconceptions pertains to the true nature and character of God; the other is a misunderstanding of the deity of Christ.

All major cults and heresy within the church have one or both of these issues in common.[102] For instance, Mormons teach that Jesus is the Savior, while claiming that God was once a man like them and that one day they too will become gods like him.[103] The belief that God was once a man just like them is to do much injustice to the true character of God, not elevating Him to the creator of the universe but relegating Him to the status of a mere man.[104] Mormonism is a polytheistic religion with a belief in many gods.

---

[102] Charles Caldwell Ryrie, *A Survey of Bible Doctrine* (Chicago: Moody Press, 1972).

[103] Prophet Joseph Smith Jr., *King Follett Discourse*, Journal of Discovery, Vol. 6: 3–4.

[104] Paul S. Karleen, *The Handbook to Bible Study: With a Guide to the Scofield Study System* (New York: Oxford University Press, 1987), 207.

Even though they may admit that Jesus is God, it has to be taken in context with their teachings that there are many gods of which Jesus was just one. They believe that one day they too will be a "god," just like Jesus. This is to do an injustice to the deity of Jesus. It is a classic case where both of these misconceptions are present in one group.[105]

Muslims are monotheistic and teach that Jesus was a prophet but not divine. Buddhists believe he was a great teacher, but it ends there.[106] Many other groups also teach he was a great teacher, master, holy man, guru, or someone to mimic and follow. Sadly many today who call themselves Christians will also say He is Savior, Redeemer, Son of God, even divine, but draw the line at admitting that He is indeed God. Mormons now claim to be Christians, as do Jehovah's Witnesses. Many other groups also lay claim to believe in Jesus but deny His divinity. Jesus said in Matthew 7:21–23 (KJV): "Not everyone that saith unto me, Lord, Lord, shall enter into the kingdom of heaven; but he that doeth the will of my Father which is in heaven." This is closely followed by: "Many will say to me in that day, Lord, Lord, have we not prophesied in thy name? and in thy name have cast out devils? And in thy name done many wonderful works? And then will I profess unto them, I never knew you: depart from me, ye that work iniquity (Mt 7:22-23)."

What we need to understand is that according to Dangana the divinity of Jesus Christ is the heart and bedrock of Christianity, and the scriptures are centered on this.[107] While McKee expresses his thought by saying that Jesus didn't come to teach us the good news; He was the good news. The gospel revolves around Him and who

---

[105]   Walter Martin, *Kingdom of the Cults* (Minneapolis, MN: Bethany Fellowhip Publishers, 1977), 179.

[106]   John Bowker, *World Religions: The Great Faiths Explored & Explained* (New York: D. K. Publishing, 2206), 59–81.

[107]   Pastor Yohanna M. Dangana, Executive Secretary Seventh-day Adventist Church, North West Nigeria Conference. Forward from the book by Solomon AkHimien: Is Jesus Christ God? A Concise Apology Satisfying the Gratuitous Dispute, Kindle edition.

He is. When we reject Him we reject God. If we deny His deity then we deny God Himself. When we reject God's revelation of Himself through Jesus Christ we deny and pervert the gospel.[108]

When we appreciate that Christ is the central figure of the Bible we recognize what the Bible is about. The Old Testament promises the coming of Christ, stating the reasons for this, way back in the beginning of Genesis (Gn 3). Throughout the rest of the Old Testament are prophecies of His birth and ministry to come. The Jews were earnestly and eagerly looking forward to the coming of their Messiah. The New Testament, on the other hand, points back to the promises fulfilled by His birth, ministry, death, and resurrection and then points us forward once again to His return. The Bible is about Jesus from the very beginning to the end.

This disagreement over the deity of Jesus is not something that is just peculiar to our own age but has been around since the first century. Many down through the ages, such as the Ebionites and others, have denied the deity of Christ. The Ebionites, during the first and second centuries, denied and rejected the divinity of Jesus, insisting that Jesus was only human and that he was created.[109] The Docetists denied the reality of His humanity, feeling that He was simply a phantomlike appearance of God. Apollianarians claimed that His humanity was incomplete.[110] The Unitarians declared Him to be adopted as divine at His baptism, while today Jehovah's Witnesses still claim He was God's highest created representative. Barhthians, on the other hand, hold that He was fully human (complete with a sin nature) and that God worked through this man to reveal Himself, especially at the cross.[111]

---

[108] Mike McKee, *Jesus Is God: He always was and always will be,* introduction, Kindle Books.

[109] Solomon S. Akhimien, *Is Jesus Christ God?* A Concise Apology Satisfying the Gratuitous dispute, Kindle edition.

[110] Earle E. Cairns, *Christianity Through the Ages,* 3rd ed (Grand Rapids, MI: Zondervan, 1981), 129–30.

[111] Charles Caldwell Ryrie.

Now many people will tell you that Jesus never said he was God. Some scholars such as Hicks will even say that the historical Jesus never claimed to be God. Therefore Hick explains that the historians of the time concluded that if Jesus did not claim to be God, then we shouldn't either.[112] The problem with this view is that if Jesus didn't claim equality with God, then why were the Jews of the day so intent on killing Him? Maybe the rest of the people didn't comprehend what Jesus was saying, but the Jews certainly did. As a result they hated Him for what they perceived as blasphemy. This is rightly so, because Jesus did claim equality with God.

As mentioned, in the very beginning of the church the doctrine of Christ's divinity came under attack. Peter Kreeft says, "as incredulous as it was to the Gentiles it was downright scandalous to the Jews. To even consider that this man Jesus, born of a woman just like any other man, could be God was the most frivolous, far-fetched, absurd, crazy idea ever conceived."[113]

Scripture and eyewitnesses' testimony tell us that He suffered, He bled, He hurt, He grieved, and He loved and was loved. Then He was killed and put in another man's tomb. Why? Simply because of the claims He made about Himself, not because of any evil or sin He had done.

When the divinity of Jesus is spoken of, what exactly does that mean? Wasn't Jesus just a man? Was He like the Roman pantheon of gods—half man, half god? A demigod?[114] Was He part God or a part of God as those in Eastern Mysticism would say? Was He just one of many gods as the Mormons and Hindus claim? Was He a hybrid of some long-lost alien civilization as is being tossed around

---

[112] John Hick, *The Metaphor of God Incarnate* (Louisville, KY: Knox Press, 1993), 27.

[113] Peter Kreeft, *Fundamentals of the Faith: Essays in Christian Apologetics* (San Francisco: Ignatius Press, 1988), 59.

[114] John Wesley, *Sermons, on Several Occasions* (Oak Harbor, WA: Logos Research Systems, 1999).

today? Some superangel?[115] Or maybe He was just another superhero, the stuff of legends and imaginations of men, which we are so fond of today.

One thing that seems to evade many today is that Jesus was born a Jew. The Jews did not have a pantheon of gods as the surrounding nations did. They did not believe God was intertwined with all of His creation as pantheism claims. Pantheism teaches that the divine essence is in everything, and everything is a part of the divine. On the contrary, Jews believed their God (singular) was the creator of heaven and earth. He was transcendent and set apart from His creation, yet active and sovereign in all its functions. This is especially so in His dealings with humankind, which leaves them with the question of how Jesus could conceivably be a god, let alone the one true God. Who was this man called Jesus, and what are we to believe of Him?

In order for us to have the correct response to Him we must have a firm grasp of who He was and is. Was He a mere mortal, or was He God, the creator of the universe? One demands our respect and worship and allegiance. The other does not.

Again, Kreeft says that for most scholars their first line of defense against the divinity of Christ is by an all out attack on the historical reliability and accuracy of scripture, particularly where it pertains to the gospels.[116] Miles McKee might chime in with the thought that in order to redeem the lost, God Himself became flesh and blood to die on the cross for sinners, which is somewhat ironic when you figure that He was the creator of heaven and earth and all living things.[117]

C. S. Lewis would pose this question called the trilemma. Either Jesus was who He claimed to be, which was Lord, or He was a liar or a lunatic. According to Lewis, for a man to make the claims Jesus did and know they were not true would make Him a liar, not to mention

---

[115] J. I. Packer, *Growing in Christ* (Wheaton, IL: Crossway Books, 1994).
[116] Kreeft, 59.
[117] Miles McKee, 2.

a very bad man. On the other hand, if Jesus believed the things He said of Himself, and they were not true, then He was plainly deluded or at worst a lunatic. So we are left with the alternative that, as ridiculous as it may sound, He must be Lord.[118]

Even that fictional detective of international fame Sherlock Holmes would have this to say: "No matter how ridiculous something may appear, if every alternative proves false we must go with the obvious."[119] Some have viewed C. S. Lewis's statement as oversimplified. Bart Ehrman, for instance, would go so far as to suggest there might even be a fourth category to add to Lewis's observation, which could be likened to folklore or legend passed down by oral tradition based on eyewitness accounts, which he believed was unreliable due to memory studies he had undertaken.[120] Was Jesus just a legend or a myth? The scriptures would tell us otherwise based not only on what Jesus said of Himself but what His closest followers would have to say concerning Him.

Due to our limited space we cannot even begin a complete study of Christology. Nor do we intend to delve into the nature of the Trinity. Both of these doctrines are of extreme importance to be sure. However, they are way beyond the scope of this particular study. There are two questions of importance to the believer that we want to investigate: (1) Did Jesus actually make the claim of being God? and (2) Did the disciples, Paul, and the early church believe Him to be God? We may not obtain all the answers we seek, but we should find enough to satisfy the question once and for all.

As Christians we believe in the Trinity. The godhead consisting of the Father, Son, and Holy Spirit—coeternal, coexistent, and coequal. God the father, God the Son, and God the Holy Spirit

---

[118] C. S. Lewis, *Mere Christianity* (New York: Harper One, 1952), 54–56.

[119] Sir Arthur Conan Doyle, *Sherlock Holmes: The sign of the Four* (Double Day, 1890), 111. His famous quote is: "When you have eliminated the impossible, whatever remains, however improbably, must be the truth."

[120] Bart Erhman, *Jesus before the Gospels* (New York: Harper Collins, 2016), 10–13.

equal one God—three persons as one God, which is very basic and simple and about as far as we are going to go into the actual trinity. This is just for the sake of clarification as we move into our study.

As Christians we are not polytheist, we are monotheist. We believe in only one God. "Hear, O Israel: The LORD our God is one LORD (Deut 6:4 KJV). There are three distinct persons within the godhead. So when we talk of Jesus being God, it is with full understanding of the Trinity—not as separate gods or subgods to the Almighty but all part and parcel of the one God. Just so we don't get ourselves confused, we have gotten that out of the way.

Now regardless of what we may believe, that we know. We first and foremost need to know what God's word says. Did Jesus claim to be God, or was this a fabrication of later generations as claimed by Ehrman?[121] Did the early church believe Jesus to be God in the flesh? Did John, James, Peter, and Paul? Let's take a look and see what we can find out.

Two Natures of Christ

So who or what was Jesus? Well, scripture plainly states He took on human form, being born of a human woman (Phil 2, prologue of John 1:1–18) in the incarnation. He was flesh and blood just like everyone else born on earth. Ryrie says that He bled, He hurt, He got tired and hungry, He thirsted, and He died (Jn 4). He had joys, and He experienced loss and sorrows, just as all the rest of humans on earth experience in their lifetime. He was 100 percent man, with one single difference; He was without sin, and no other human being has that characteristic.[122]

---

[121] Ehrman, *Jesus Before the Gospels* (New York: Harper Collins, 2016), 10–13.

[122] Charles Caldwell Ryrie, *A Survey of Bible Doctrine* (Chicago: Moody Press, 1972).

Unlike Adam, He was not born with a sinful nature. He was tempted like us (1 Cor 15). Yet He didn't succumb to the temptation as Adam did. He was impeccable (without defect) as only God Himself is. This doesn't mean He couldn't sin; it relates more in terms of He did not sin. According to Shedd, "His temptations were not to see if He could sin, but to prove that He could not. Nevertheless, the temptations were real, 'for the reality of a test does not lie in the moral nature of the one tested or in the ability to yield to it." [123]

It is interesting to note that He was human, for a human can die. We know that God is eternal and as a result cannot die, ever. Now since He lived here on earth as a man, He identifies with and sympathizes with us as our priest. As Ryric pointed out: "We must remember that His humanity was always perfect" (Heb 4:15, 2 Cor 5:21). [124]

He was not some half man, half god of Greek or Roman mythology. This would infer that He was 50 percent divine and 50 percent human. Some may conclude that maybe He was just a little bit man and a little bit God, which sounds more like a sad country-western song. Maybe the term God-man is more applicable, as it implies God in the form of man, which correlates beautifully with Philippians 2:5–8. After all, His divinity is the most important aspect of His nature. If He was mere man and not God, then none of this would matter; His death would have meant nothing except as another martyr. He could not have forgiven our sin or raised the dead or stilled the storm. Only if He is God does any of this apply. [125]

What we do know from scripture is that Jesus was not only fully man but that He was also fully God, all at the same time. It was also of utmost importance that Christ be fully human. Not half human like some hybrid but totally human. How else could God so

---

[123] William G. Shedd. *Dogmatic Theology* 3rd ed. (Phillipsburg, NJ: R&R Publishing, 2003), 33, 662–64.

[124] Charles Caldwell Ryrie.

[125] Shedd, 669.

readily relate to humanity? How can this be? Well, admittedly this is a mystery. There are some things God just doesn't tell us or intend for us to know the full extent of. Our job is to search the scriptures and see if these things are true in accordance with scriptures. The disciples searched the scriptures and in them found Jesus (Jn 5:39).

Now here we are with what appears to be an enigma. We have this man, Jesus, and He is 100 percent human. At the same time this same Jesus is 100 percent God. There is a theological term for it, and that is the "hypostatic union." This means that two natures are joined in one—one divine, one natural, all in the same person. This question of deity and humanity being united in Jesus has been debated throughout church history. It is one of those glorious mysteries of the Bible. Not just that. It is also the heart of the gospel—the good news that God took on the form of a man and came down to reconcile us to Him. Isn't it interesting that God came down to reconcile humankind to Himself? Never does the Bible say that God reconciles Himself to us. We are the ones indebted to Him.

Speaking about the sacrifice on the cross, Shedd had this to say: "For, it was a requisite that the mediator should be God, that he might sustain and keep the human nature from sinking under the infinite wrath of God and the power of death" (Westminster Larger Catechism, 38). "In so doing He showed that He is Lord and conqueror of Satan and his kingdom" (Col 2:15; Ps 2:2, 4; 1 Cor 15:25; Heb 2:10). To paraphrase in explaining His humanity, the Redeemer of sinful men must be truly human, just not given to their weakness. He couldn't be a fallen man, meaning He would have to be without sin. He was the ideal man, not the actual sinful creation that man had become through sin. As a human He would be temptable, yet not give in to sin. He had to be truly human in order to be assailable by temptation so that He would be able to sympathize with every tempted man. He could not be weak or sinful because He was "mighty to save," traveling in the greatness of His strength (Is 63:1). He had to have the power to overcome all temptation (Heb 2:18). Because fallen and helpless man cannot trust himself to one who is himself liable to fall."[126]

Ryrie stated: "Orthodoxy has always taught that Jesus was fully God and perfect man and that these two natures were united in one person without forming a third nature (as Eutychius said) or two separate persons (as Nestorius taught)." [127]

It is interesting that this combination of God and man didn't constitute a third nature. It didn't come together and form a new life-form: Nor did the two mix together becoming diluted or compromised in any way. Instead they were two very distinct, pure natures in one person. Hodges has this to say regarding the two natures.

In the Westminster Confession it states that God and the Son were perfectly joined as one person, there was no "conversion, composition, or confusion." While His humanity of Jesus was formed in Mary's womb, "His divinity is eternal and personal where His humanity is impersonal."[128]

Jesus didn't start His existence as a man. He Is God: He is eternal: He is the Alpha and Omega, without beginning or end: He always was, always is, and always will be. Yet for a time He set that all aside, and He became human (Phil 2:6 8). Does this mean He gave up His divinity when He became man? No, He still retained all of the attributes of God. It was just that He was willing to harness or subdue them when He walked among us.[129]

In the little village of Bethlehem, God stepped down from heaven into time and a space. In so doing He became the only advocate between sinful man and a holy God. Why was this necessary? Humankind had no representative before an offended God. Humankind the offenders could not atone for sin simply due

126 Shedd, 669–70.
127 Charles Caldwell Ryrie.
128 A. A. Hodges, *The Westminster Confession: A Commentary*, chapter 8: "Of Christ the Mediator," section, P cii.
129 Shedd, 670.

to the fact that they are humans. As such, all humans under Adam have inherited a sin nature. Therefore no human could atone for his or her own or anyone else's sin. Only the one who is without sin could accomplish this, and God Himself is the only one who is sinless and holy. One doesn't want to stand before a holy God without an advocate to speak for him. No more so than we would want to stand before a judge in a courtroom without a defense attorney beside us. We are sinners because it is our nature, thanks to Adam's sin. We are basically our own worst enemy. We needed and still need a Savior even in our "enlightened" age.[130]

John 1:29 (NIV) states: "Behold the Lamb of God which takes away the sin of the world." The blood of lambs and goats did not forgive men their; sins it simply covered their sins. In Exodus12:13, the blood applied on the door posts was able to protect only those who took refuge under it. The blood of bulls and goats was never meant to be anything but a temporary covering until the Messiah came. A greater sacrifice was required to appease God. With humankind being unable to atone for their own sins, only God Himself was qualified. Even the angels in heaven were not competent for something of this magnitude. Only God can forgive sin, no one else on earth or in heaven has that ability.

What Did Jesus Say about Himself?

While some may claim that Jesus never claimed to be God, He certainly did infer such, if not blatantly proclaim it.[131] It's just that so much of what He said and did just went right over most folks' heads, with the exception of the Jews and the Pharisees, who knew

---

[130] Jack Hibbs, *Real Life with Jack Hibbs* broadcast (Cedar City, UT: Crossover Radio 88.9, 2017).

[131] Biblical Studies Press, *The NET Bible First Edition Notes* (Biblical Studies Press, 2006), 2 Pt 3:12–13. Logos.

perfectly well what He was saying. They became so infuriated that they plotted to kill Jesus themselves (Jn 11:53).

The "I AM" Sayings of Jesus

Probably the first thing to come to mind is the seven "I AM" of Jesus. Again we have to understand this from a Jewish perspective, or this will just float right over our heads too. For a man to even apply the term "I AM" to himself was in itself flagrant blasphemy. Jesus said it seven times. To the Jews this was a sacred term applied only to God Himself. When God revealed Himself for the first time to Moses in the wilderness (Ex 3:14 KJV) He revealed Himself as the I AM THAT I AM. In other words, He just is; He always was; He always will be. This then illustrates to us that when Jesus makes the claims of the I AM statements that He is in effect making an assertion of equality with God.[132] Let's take a look at them.

- "I am the Bread of Life" (Jn 6:35 KJV).
- "I am the light of the world" (Jn 8:12 KJV). First John 1:5 (NIV) states that. The same thing is said of the Father. "God is light and in Him is no darkness at all." David says in Psalm 27:1 (NIV): "The Lord is my light and my salvation."
- "I AM the way, the truth and the life" (Jn 14:6). Not a way or another way, but the only way, truth and life. "The," being the definite article here, singles this out very clearly.
- "I Am the good shepherd" (Jn 10:11). Again the Old Testament in Psalm 23:1 says God is my shepherd. Hebrews 13:20 speaks of the God of peace that brought again from the dead our Lord Jesus, that great shepherd of the sheep through the blood of the everlasting covenant.
- "I Am the door or gate for the sheep to enter" (Jn 10:7).

---

[132] Paul. S. Karleen, *The Handbook to Bible Study: With a Guide to the Scofield Study System* (New York: Oxford University Press, 1987), 334–35.

- "I AM the resurrection and the life" (Jn 11:25–26). Jesus is the fountain of life and the head and author of the resurrection.[133]
- "I am the vine" (Jn 15:5 KJV).

There are a few more "I AM" statements that Jesus made such as:

- I Am the Alpha and Omega (Rv 1:7, 22:12–13). Jesus made this claim of Himself. This is a divine name. Isaiah 44:6 says: "Thus saith the LORD the King of Israel and his redeemer the LORD of hosts; I am the first, and I am the last; and beside me there is not God." Then again, speaking of Jesus, Revelation 1:8 (KJV) says: "I am Alpha and Omega, the beginning and the ending saith the Lord, which is, and was, and which is to come the Almighty." Isaiah 41:4 says: "Who hath wroth and done it, calling the generations from the beginning: I the LORD, the first, and with the last; I am."
- He states to the Jews in another place: "Verily, Verily I say to you, before Abraham, I Am" (Jn 8:58). Note that He did not say "I was," but "I Am."

Many times Jesus claimed equality with God and to have a unique relationship with the Father. Even the use of the term "My Father" was taken by the Jews to mean a clear claim to divinity. Thus, Jesus was yet again claiming His equality with God.[134] As He mentioned, He and the father were one (Jn 10:30). Utley states very plainly that this statement was not just referring to a biological

[133] Keith Brooks, *Summarized Bible: Complete Summary of the New Testament* (Bellingham, WA: Logos Bible Software, 2009).
[134] M. S. Mills, *The Life of Christ: A Study Guide to the Gospel Record* (Dallas, TX: 3E Ministries, 1999).

or generational fashion, but in the very essence of their being.[135] He was the *only* begotten of the father. There were no siblings of like manner. He was the one and only unique Son of God. The term "Son of God" did not necessarily imply physical descent as one might be inclined to assume. "The title describes His deity."[136] This was one of the factors that so infuriated the Jews. Those who would later come to faith in Christ would also be called the "Sons of God" (Jn 1:12). It would be by adoption through faith in Christ, never to be confused with the same essence or relationship as Jesus had with the Father.

Godly Attributes

We have to ask: Did Jesus retain any of the attributes of the Father while He was on earth? Does Philippians 2:6–8 tell us that Christ emptied Himself of some or all aspects of His deity when He came to earth? We know, according to verse 6, that He possessed all the attributes of deity before the incarnation. So then why do we assume He gave them all up while in the flesh? We know that He continued to subsist in the form of God. Does this mean then that it was possible that even during the incarnation He continued to subsist in the form of God? The word *form* means not external accidents but essential attributes of deity. From this we learn that He was not simply appearing as God: He truly was God. He merely took on the form of a servant. He wasn't someone (a man) who took upon Himself the form of God. Rather He was God who humbled Himself by taking on the form of a man, even that of a lowly servant.[137]

---

[135] Robert James Utley, vol. 4, *The Beloved Disciple's Memoirs and Letters: The Gospel of John, I, II, and III John*, Study Guide Commentary Series (Marshall, TX: Bible Lessons International, 1999).

[136] Paul S. Karleen.

[137] Charles Caldwell Ryrie.

The word translated *nature* is crucial to the passage in verses 6 and 7. The Greek is *morphe,* and it means to transform. This word *form* in the KJV and NASB stresses the inner essence or reality of that with which it is associated. Paul said that Christ Jesus "is the very essence (morphe) of God. And in His incarnation He embraced perfect humanity. His complete and absolute deity is here carefully stressed by the apostle. This claim, of course, enraged the Jewish leaders (Jn 5:18).

Even so, Christ did not consider His equality with God (Phil 2:6–8) something to be held onto. He did not hesitate to set aside His self-willed use of deity when He became a man. As God He had all the rights of that deity, and yet He surrendered His right to manifest Himself visibly as the God of all splendor and glory.[138] The word *emptied* comes from the Greek word *kenoo.* It points to the divesting of His self-interests but not His deity. Although He became a man to serve others and His humanity was genuine and complete, He was different from all other humans due to His being sinless (Heb 4:15).[139]

Again Ryrie says that if our Lord had surrendered some of His divine attributes while here on earth, "then His essential character would have been changed, and He would not have been fully God while on earth." It is impossible to subtract any attributes without changing the character of the person. Usually those who do, take away the "omni" attributes (omniscience, omnipotence, omnipresence). Yet we know that Christ possessed these attributes during His incarnation. All we have to do is look at Matthew 28:18 (KJV): "And Jesus came and spoke to them saying, All power is given unto me in heaven and in earth" (omnipotence). Then we

---

[138]   Robert P. Lightner, "Philippians" *in The Bible Knowledge Commentary: An Exposition of the Scriptures,* ed. J. F. Walvoord and R. B. Zuck (Wheaton, IL: Victor Books, 1985), Phil 2:6–8.

[139]   John F. Walvoord and Roy B. Zuck, *The Bible Knowledge Commentary: An Exposition of the Scriptures,* by Dallas Seminary Faculty, based on NIV. E-Sword.

have Matthew 18:20, where Jesus says: "For where two or three are gathered together in my name, there am I in the midst of them (omnipresence)." In Mark 2:8 (KJV) Jesus said, "And immediately when Jesus perceived in His spirit that they so reasoned within themselves, He said unto them, Why reason ye these things in your hearts" (omniscience). So, we can see from these three verses that He was still operating within His divine attributes.

Therefore when people say He emptied Himself of His divine attributes while on earth simply because He could have called ten thousand angels to His rescue and didn't, they seem to be missing the real point. Just because He didn't call them didn't mean that they were not immediately available to Him as God. Ryrie says that if "Christ surrendered His attributes at the incarnation this is in direct conflict with scriptural evidence concerning His person during the incarnation."[140]

We also know that He was omnipotent because He calmed the sea. He walked on water, which means He had the power to not just transform the water into a hard surface but had the ability to transform the molecular structure of the water itself, just as He did when He turned the water into wine at the wedding in Cana. He had the power to feed over five thousand men, with only two fish and five little loaves of bread.

Ephesians 1:19–23 (KJV) speaks of God's mighty power:

- "Which he wrought in Christ, when he raised Him from the dead, and set him at his own right hand in the heavenly places" (v. 20; also Acts 2:24).
- "Far above all principalities and power, and might, and dominion, and every name that is named, not only in this world, but also in that which is to come" (v. 21; also Phil 2:9).

---

[140] Ryrie.

- "And hath put all things under his feet, and gave him to be the head over all things to the church" (v. 22).
- "Which is his body, the fullness of him that filleth all in all" (v. 23).

Whereas in Hebrews 1:3 He is said to uphold all things by the word of His power.

He had the power to heal all diseases. He raised the dead (Jn 11:25). He cleansed the lepers. He forgave sin (which was only something God could do) He was all knowing (omniscient) as He knew what Nathaniel was doing under the fig tree (Jn 1:48). He knew the history of the woman at the well, whom He had never met before (Jn 4:17–18). He was omnipresent; He said before Abraham was I AM, meaning, He was there (Jn 8:58). He claimed to be the Alpha and Omega, the beginning and the end (omnipresent) (Rv 1:17).

Having risen from the dead proved His eternal nature. Plus He claimed on more than one occasion to be the Alpha and Omega, the beginning and the end of all things. His very nature was love and mercy. Yet He claimed that He was to be the judge who would judge the nations and everyone in them, speaking of His sovereignty (Jn 5:27). Still He emptied Himself to come to earth as a human; He still retained or had access to His divinity or His equality with God. He did not sin; He was Righteous, and yet we are told there are none righteous but God. He was impeccable, without sin or a sin nature, yet fully human with the ability to fall into sin. Yet it was because of this impeccability that only He could die for our sin. He was the Prince of Peace.

We can see from this short list that Jesus did possess many of God's attributes.

- His holiness, righteousness
- Sovereignty
- Omnipotence

- Omniscience
- Omnipresence
- Eternal
- Immutable

Early Church and Apostles

Did the early disciples and apostles believe Jesus was God? Peter did. When He proclaimed that Jesus was the Christ, the Son of the Living God, He believed it. Thomas, after seeing the resurrected Christ, abandoned all doubt and proclaimed it (Jn 20:28). As did all the rest of the disciples, not to mention all the rest that saw Jesus before His ascension. Luke says that there were not a few but many Pharisees and scribes who believed after the resurrection.

In Acts 7, Stephen saw the resurrected Christ seated at the right hand of God, in that special place of power moments before His death.

Paul also, that great champion of the faith, who stood by as Stephen was stoned and approved of this act. He too talked about the deity of Christ after having His own encounter with Jesus of Nazareth. In 1 Corinthians 2:8 (KJV), Paul speaks of Christ Jesus as the Lord of glory: "Which none of the princes of this world knew: for had they known it, they would not have crucified the Lord of glory." When Paul wrote to the Colossians to speak of God's redemptive working in their lives, he had much to say concerning the exaltation and preeminence of Christ. In verses 15–20 of chapter 1 he mentions "seven unique characteristics of Christ, which fittingly qualify Him to have the supremacy. Christ is: (1) the image of God, (2) the firstborn over Creation, (3) Creator of the universe, (4) head of the church, (5) firstborn from the dead, (6) the fullness of God, (7) the Reconciler of all things. No other list shows so many characteristics of Christ and His deity. Christ is the supreme

Sovereign of the universe."[141] In Colossians 2:9 (KJV), Paul says "For in him (Jesus) dwelleth all the fullness of the Godhead bodily."

R. A. Torrey says there can be no mistaking that this "Lord of glory' is Jehovah God.[142] Psalm 24:8–10 (KJV) says:

> Who is this king of glory? The LORD strong and mighty, the LORD mighty in battle. "Lift up your heads, O ye gates; even lift them up, ye everlasting doors; and the King of glory shall come in. Who is this King of glory? The LORD of hosts, he is the King of glory. Selah.

None were as adamant about the deity of Jesus as John.[143] His prologue alone is so poignant in its description of the Word of God made flesh. This theme of Jesus as LORD is carried throughout all of his epistles and into the revelation and future events.

Let us not forget the testimony of Thomas, who confessed to Jesus, "My LORD and my God" (Jn 20:28–29). Rather than rebuking Thomas for idolatry, Jesus accepted His worship that was due only to God. All the disciples who saw the resurrected Christ believed He was deity. If Jesus claimed to be the king of glory, then He had to be Jehovah God.

---

[141] Norman L. Geisler, "Colossians" in *The Bible Knowledge Commentary: An Exposition of the Scriptures,* ed. J. F. Walvoord and R. B. Zuch (Wheaton, IL: Victor Books, 1985), Col 1:15–20.

[142] R. A. Torrey. Kindle ed.

[143] Eugene E. Carpenter and Philip W. Comfort, *Holman Treasury of Key Bible Words: 200 Greek and 200 Hebrew Words Defined and Explained* (Nashville, TN: Broadman & Holman, 2000).

Conclusion

Therefore, what are we to think on this subject today? Has the message changed? Was He Lord back then in the first century, but not today in the twenty-first? Hardly. In Hebrews 13:8 the writer says that "Jesus is the same yesterday, today and forever." This speaks of God's attribute of immutability as well as His eternal nature.

This is a very brief look at a very intense subject. Yet, it gives us a glimpse of some of the reasons for the belief that Jesus is Jehovah God. Although we can never begin to comprehend how it is that Jesus could be 100 percent God at the same time He was 100 percent man, we know this is true. It is solidly taught within the pages of scripture. God came to live with us, so that He could save us, because of the great love He had for us.

Jesus was not just divine; He was deity. Therefore the subject seems to be not the divinity of Jesus, because it is not a matter of whether Jesus was divine, but rather, is Jesus Christ God? "The Doctrine of the deity of Jesus Christ formed the very warp and woof of the Bible."[144]

He was born of a virgin in a little town called Bethlehem. They called His name Jesus, as He came to save His people. He was called Immanuel, "God with us." The magnitude of this is such that it is no wonder that it turned the world upside down. It is the good news to the entire world that a Savior had come to save them from their sin. Only God could do that and no one less. In the words of Kreeft and Tacelli, if Christ really is divine, then the incarnation—birth of Christ—is the most important event in history. All of history hinges upon this one thing. It changed everything. He explains how heaven's gate was closed because of sin. When Christ died on the cross it was reopened for the first time in history, making this the

---

[144] R.A. Torrey, *The deity of Jesus Christ* (1856–1928) Kindle Ed.

most important event in history.[145] This is truly shown in the rent veil over the holy of holies and how humans once again had access to the throne of God through faith in Jesus.

As we begin to study and understand the nature and character of God, especially in regard to His holiness, and then do likewise and come to the conclusion that Jesus although fully human was also God in the flesh. Theological orthodoxy is the person of Christ. Both His deity and His humanity must be affirmed, or the entire doctrine of salvation is affected. Only a Jesus who is truly God and truly man can provide a complete salvation for humanity.[146]

He also was sinless and holy. We can now begin to realize that He also has called us to be holy. Now we can never be holy as Jesus was because we are all born under the curse of sin. Jesus was not. But He has given us His Holy Spirit to live within us, and it is through His grace and mercy that we can begin to lay aside sin and truly start to live in a manner pleasing to the master. Let us move on into the subject of obedience and how it affects our lives.

Then again, Kreeft and Tacelli would reply that if Jesus is divine, then He should have control and access to our entire lives and all of our thoughts. That in turn would be our obligation to Him. We must believe what He says and obey all that He commands. To be free is to conform to Him because He is divine.[147] From this we learn that to Jesus we owe all of our faith, trust, allegiance, and worship unto God our savior.

---

[145]   Peter Kreeft and Ronald K. Tacelli, *Handbook of Christian Apologetics: Hundreds of Answers to Crucial Questions* (Downers Grove, IL: Intervarsity Press, 1994), 152.

[146]   James P. Eckman, *Exploring Church History* (Wheaton, IL: Crossway, 2002), 32.

[147]   Kreeft and Tacelli, 152.

5
CHAPTER

Holiness and Obedience

God's character is saturated with His holiness. Every attribute of His character is a holy attribute. We also know that Jesus and the Holy Spirit are holy. In God's word, God calls us to be holy, as does Jesus in the Gospels and the apostles in the epistles. The Holy Spirit Himself prompts us to holy behavior through His Word, the Bible (1 Pt 1:16). Therefore we realize our need as Christians to be holy as He is.

How will we find good? George Eliot says that "it is not so much a choice as it is a river coursing outward from the invisible throne. This river of holiness flows primarily by the means of obedience."[148]

As followers of Jesus we want to find and do that which is pleasing to our Lord. The Bible ties obedience to success in the Old Testament. When God promised to give the land to the Israelites,

---

[148] Herschel H. Hobbs, *My Favorite Illustrations* (Nashville, TN: Broadman Press, 1990), Logos.

it was based on their obedience to Him. The experiences of their fathers during the forty years in the desert gave testimony to the importance of their compliance. Add that to the fact that they were to do "all of the law," not just the laws with which they agreed. God would not be satisfied with partial obedience.[149]

What could possibly lead us to believe obedience is no longer important? Is it simply because we are now under grace? On the contrary, we still need to learn obedience. Obedience is the key to pleasing God—not only as individuals but also within the body of Christ. Obedience to what? His word. Hebrews 12:14 (NIV) states: "Without Holiness no man shall see the Lord." Yes, this was written to the Christians of the day. In James 4:8 when speaking of the sin within the church, James told them: "Draw near to God, and he will draw nigh to you. Cleanse your hands, ye sinners; and purify your hearts, ye double minded." Is something different expected of the church today? Do we not have divisions in the church warring against one another? Has immorality been erased in the church today? Are pride and personal ambition just problems in Old Testament days, or is it still something with which to grapple? Has gossip been abandoned along with slander, lying, and stealing, not to mention plain, ordinary, everyday sin?

God has something better in mind for the Christian. In Psalms 24:3–5 (KJV), the psalmist asks this question: "Who shall ascent into the hill of the LORD? Or who shall stand in his holy place? He that hath clean hands, and a pure heart; who hath not lifted up his soul unto vanity, nor sworn deceitfully. He shall receive the blessing from the LORD, and righteousness from the God of his salvation."

We can see from these scripture references that with our free gift of salvation by grace there is a responsibility on the believers' part, and that is called obedience. Storm says the only route to a deeper

---

[149] Roger Ellsworth, *Opening Up Joshua: Opening Up Commentary* (Leonminster: Day One Publications, 2008), 35.

experience of God's love is by the route of holiness. This requires clean hands as well as a clean heart.[150]

Overall, the church today is lacking a healthy fear of God because all reverence and fear is gone. This needs to change. The image many have today of God is that of a big love bunny, where He loves us so much that nothing we can do offends or grieves Him. We have in essence turned Him into a God of our liking as opposed to who He actually is—the Almighty, the Holy, and the Just God of Abraham, Isaac, and Jacob. Yes, He loves us His word assures us of that. Calvary itself is the proof of this (Jn 3:16, Rom 5:8). Just so we could once again have fellowship with Him. We just need to remember that it was us in our sin that offended this holy and righteous God. Therefore if we continue in that sin after having been saved, we should never be deceived into believing that our sin will not insult Him or cause Him to mourn. We can, according to scripture, offend the Holy Spirit (who is God). In Ephesians 4:30, Paul tells us not to grieve the Holy Spirit with which we are sealed unto the day of redemption.

To grieve means to burden or cause someone to sorrow. While the meaning of offend means to transgress or break the moral or divine law. Therefore when we grieve someone it signifies causing them difficulty, discomfort, injury, dislike, anger, vexation, or hurt.[151]

In Isaiah 63:10 we are told that the Israelites, whom God loved and carried all the days of old, rebelled and grieved (vexed) His Holy Spirit. This is interesting because this is from the Hebrew word for grieve which is *atsab, aw-tsab,* which takes us back to the meaning of offend—namely to rebuke, hurt, distress, vex, or to be made sorry.[152]

---

[150] Andrew Storm, *True and False Revival* (Revival School Press, 2008).

[151] Merriam-Webster, *Merriam-Webster's Collegiate Dictionary, eleventh ed.* (Springfield, MA: Merriam-Webster, 2003).

[152] James Strong, *A Concise Dictionary of the Words in the Greek Testament and the Hebrew Bible* (Bellingham, WA: Logos Bible Software, 2009).

We can see from these scriptures that it is possible to offend (hurt or grieve) God by our behavior, speech, or attitudes. If we have been truly born again, we don't want to do this. We want as Christians to live our lives in a manner that is pleasing to God but not because we have to in order to secure our salvation. That is already secure in Christ. We want to do it because of a heart change that has taken place in our lives. We do it because we love Him and therefore want to please Him.

If a person claims to be a Christian yet is still living as he or she did before coming to Christ, or maybe worse, then there is something terribly wrong with that person's testimony. John Owens put it like this: "Being born again signals a definite break with the lifestyle dominated by sin."[153] It is interesting that one of the sure signs of the Holy Spirit indwelling the life of a believer is a changed life. This does not imply a perfect life but certainly a changed one.

Consequently, we do not want to live a life any longer that would be offensive to a holy God. Once we have been cleansed and set apart by the blood of Jesus Christ and had our sins forgiven, then we must consecrate ourselves to live in accordance with the law of holiness. These constitute the root of the doctrine of sanctification to which all who belong to Christ are called.[154]

Many times Christians just stick their heads in the sand like the silly ostrich, refusing to accept any responsibility for their actions. Yet we of all people should not roam around as those without knowledge.[155] It is as we learn the blessing of obedience that God opens up His word and His will unto us. Oswald affirms that even the tiniest move on our part toward obedience and the heavens open up and the "profoundest truth of God" is revealed to us. The truths

---

[153]   Dr. David Brown, *Go and Sin No More*, 95. Quote by "John Owens."

[154]   Warren W. Wiersbe, *Be Holy: "Be" Commentary Series* (Wheaton, IL: Victor Books, 1996), 17.

[155]   Robertson McQuilkin, *The Keswick Perspective: Five Views on Sanctification*(Grand Rapids, MI: Zondervan, 1987) 163.

He reveals to us will never be revealed, nor will more come, until we first learn to obey what we already know.[156]

If we want to know God's will for our lives, then we must learn to walk in obedience. In John 7:16–17 Jesus says that the doctrine He was teaching was not His own but that of the father. If a man would do His will, he would know whether or not this doctrine was of God. Basically it is saying that the only way to know God's will is to do His will.[157]

A spiritual relationship is not a gradual one in that He cleanses us from more and more sin. We are either in the light, or we are not. The question is are we walking in the light of God's love and mercy or are we walking in darkness? The choice is ours. We are the ones who have to make the decision to now live for Christ. With this decision comes much peace and contentment. At the same time we must keep in mind that the moment we turn away from obedience, darkness and death move in and start to work. The only way to get to know God's will is to obey Him in whatever He is asking. When we do His bidding and obey, then and only then will He open up and show us the next step in following Him.[158]

Difficulty

What is it about the term *obedience* that at the mere mention of it people get their backs up? Why? Is it just that we live in a society with fewer rules, where lawlessness has become more acceptable as the norm? Where the mere sight of a boundary and all we see is a

---

[156] Oswald Chambers, *My Utmost for His Highest: Selections for the Year* (Grand Rapids, MI: Oswald Chambers Publications; Marshall Pickering, 1986), "Encouragement," vv. 4–6.

[157] Oswald Chambers, *The Moral Foundation of Life: A Series of Talks on the Ethical Principle of the Christian Life* (Hants UK: Marshall, Morgan & Scott, 1936).

[158] Chamber, *My Utmost for His Highest.*

threat to our "freedom"? Laws and regulations have been put into place for our protection and benefit. They can be very beneficial and profitable if we will just follow and live in accordance with them.

What is so threatening about something as simple and basic as being obedient? Instead of rebelling against the thought of obedience, we should embrace it as something we get to do—as a rare privilege not given to others. As such we should continually ask God to break up our hard, rebellious hearts so that we might become pliable and capable of bearing fruit fitting of the Holy Spirit. As Christ's followers, we do not want any seed of rebellion or bitterness springing up within our hearts. It should be our desire to want to serve God, which means laying down our own will and lives daily to seek His will—learning to walk in discipline and obedience to His Word and Spirit.

God gave commandments to humans but not to restrict them or confine them. Rather He gave them so that our lives would be enriched (Ps 19:7–11). Now if, as the psalmist says, God gave His laws for that purpose, then why wouldn't everyone want to follow them?

In America we pride ourselves on our freedom, as we should. Slavery of any form is a terrible thing. However, slavery in one form or another has been with us since the beginning of time. When we are slaves, we belong to the one who bought us. We might say like Paul that we are also the slaves of the one we give ourselves to. While we were lost in our sin, we were slaves to that sin and to this world and to the enemy of our souls. Just because we may not have been aware of our state of slavery isn't the point. Rather it is the fact that we are all slaves of someone or something, and as a result of that we do conform to whatever or whoever that may be. In Romans 6:16–18 (KJV), Paul says:

> Know ye not, that to whom ye yield yourselves
> servants to obey, his servants ye are to whom ye
> obey; whether of sin unto death, or of obedience

unto righteousness? But God be thanked, that ye were the servants of sin, but ye have obeyed from the heart that form of doctrine which was delivered you. Being then made free from sin, ye became the servants of righteousness.

Christ on the cross paid our ransom to set us free from the slavery and bondage of sin. We have been bought with a price (Heb 9:12). When we come to Christ to have our sins forgiven, we are giving our lives to Him. He becomes our new master, and we no longer have to live in bondage under the enemy's domain. The truth is that from that time forward we no longer belong to ourselves, either. We are to crucify the flesh, according to Galatians 5:24, and die to ourselves and sin. Even Calvin when speaking of sanctification states that when the Holy Spirit takes up residence within us He destroys the lust of the flesh within us day by day. Then we become sanctified and therefore more consecrated to the Lord in "true purity of life," while our hearts grow in obedience to the law.[159]

That being the case, what should our attitude be? He has saved us from our sin and the bondage that sin brought. He has redeemed us, and our attitude should be one of total and complete gratitude, thanksgiving, praise, worship, and joy.

It is not that we have to obey. Our new attitude should be that we get to obey. What an honor and a privilege it is for a Christian to walk in obedience. For there is much blessing to follow. All one needs to do is read the book of Proverbs and see the promises God has for those who seek after Him and follow His commands. Why would a Christian ever want to do anything less? There is no middle ground here; it is all or nothing. It is either obedience or rebellion, darkness or light.

---

[159] John Calvin, *Institutes of the Christian Religion*, translated by Henry Beveridge (London: James Clark and Co., 1949) 3, 14, 10, 9.

So why is it that so many Christians still struggle with the idea of obedience? Is it because we fear it will limit us in our endeavors as Christians? Is obedience so difficult to do? Or is it simply because we are shocked that something may actually be required of us? Ravi Zacharias, commenting on Philippians 2:12–13, says that this is where "God's sovereignty and man's responsibility collide."[160] It tells us in verse 13 that God is the one who works in us and brings salvation to us. Verse 12 tells us how we are expected to work that salvation out in our everyday lives. It is a beautiful illustration of God's grace and our responsibility toward that grace—to cherish it and care for it, for the precious thing it is.

Nancy Pearcey makes the point that in the past, to be holy meant dressing according to certain standards. It meant you had to (if you were a woman) dress in dark plain clothing.[161] More than likely, this meant no frills or embellishments, as these precluded pride. Ladies were required to wear long sleeves, long skirts, long hair, high necklines, and no makeup. This certainly sounds restrictive.

It has been said one should not dance, smoke, chew, or go with girls that do. While it is true that Christians probably should not partake of these particular vices, it is not the abstention from these things that saves us. If it were, we would place ourselves right back under the law. One would spend so much time trying to figure out all that we couldn't do that we might forget what it is we were called to do in the first place. This isn't obedience or holiness; this is legalism, and we will talk more about this in another chapter. What we want is an obedience that flows naturally from the heart. It is the Christian's expression of love. So the question is how do we do this? John Wesley, speaking on his conversion experience, said he realized from the beginning there was no middle ground. It was all of his life or nothing. He stated that every area of his life was

---

[160] Ravi Zacharius, quoted from a statement he made on radio broadcast.
[161] Nancy Pearcey, *Total Truth: Liberating Christianity From Its Cultural Captivity* (Wheaton, IL: Crossway, 2008), 82.

either a sacrifice to God or to the devil. There was no room to try to serve both God and the devil. It was pretty black and white. It was either/or with nothing in between. Nothing has changed; it is still the same today.[162]

We tend to focus on the negative when the topic of holiness or obedience arises, when what we should do is rejoice, because we no longer want to do those things we did before. The truth is that the closer we come to Christ, the less we want to sin. Wesley also said, "The love of God implies total obedience."[163]

What does obedience look like? How do we manifest it in our daily walk? We are free from our former bondage; we have been born again. If we are still sinning, it is because we choose to, not because we no longer have a choice. This in itself should fill us with joy when we think of all that Christ has done for us—how He has delivered us and saved us and called us His own. The joy of the Lord should overwhelm us. This causes us to rejoice, even in the midst of life's greatest tragedies. It should cause us to be willing to stand in line (if necessary) for the opportunity to be able to serve Him. There are many blessings to the Christian who submits to the will of God. It should be understood that we do not obey Him to get what we want from Him, for that would be manipulation. Rather we serve Him out of a heart of thanksgiving.

Holiness requires obedience, and obedience requires submission to God's Word. Obedience is a verb; it is something we do. It requires discipline, and it requires action, and it requires trust on our part. Thomas Brooks stated that we shouldn't get bogged down with the duty or its difficulty. We should instead focus on being obedient to the task at hand, and let Jesus reveal Himself by making the service

---

[162] John Wesley, *A Plain Account of Christian Perfection: As believe and taught by Rev. Mr. John Wesley, from the year 1725–1777, in the works of John Wesley* (Grand Rapids, MI: Baker, 1986), vol. 11, 366.

[163] H. Ray Dunning, *Grace, Faith, & Holiness: A Wesleyan Systematic Theology* (Kansas City, MO: Beacon Hill Press, 1988), 488.

easy.[164] Jesus said His yoke was light not heavy. Obedience is not a chore; it is a joy and a privilege.

Requirements

It is interesting that Adam was only given one requirement, and He disobeyed it (Gn 2:17). It seems so innocent, but disobedience has never been incidental to God. Obedience to God demonstrates faith in God's goodness and His knowledge, and disobedience demonstrates a lack of trust.[165] It is safe to say that the more we are obedient to God, the more trust and faith we will have in Him. Like most things in life, we start out with baby steps until we are finally able to take the big steps that faith and obedience require.

Horton put it this way: "As Christians we have the responsibility to respond to both the Word and the Spirit in faith and obedience."[166]

Obedience is our expression of our worship and love for God. So often when we think of worship today we think only in terms of music. Yet, worship is so much more. It is best demonstrated through our obedience to Christ as we sing, praise, give thanks, pray, give, serve, love, and obey as we go about our daily lives.

We must learn to hear His voice and learn to distinguish His voice from the many others speaking to us. His voice is unique, and we need to learn to hear it. He expects us to do this. He says His sheep know His voice. It is interesting that sheep that have spent much time with their shepherd do know their master's voice and will respond to it. But they will not respond to a stranger (Jn 10:3–5). When people fall in love, they love the sound of their loved ones,

---

[164]   Thomas Brooks, *Precious Remedies against Satan's Devices* (1608–80) Kindle Books.

[165]   Charles R. Swindoll and Roy B. Zuck, *Understanding Christian Theology* (Nashville, TN: Thomas Nelson, 2203), 724.

[166]   Stanley M. Horton, *Five Views of Sanctification: The Pentecostal Perspective,* 123.

voice. A mother can distinguish her child's cry in the midst of a plethora of other screaming children. Why? Because they are hers, and she loves them and knows them. That is what God wants us to learn, and we only do this by spending time with Him.

It is only by establishing a personal one-on-one relationship with Him that we will be able to discern His voice from all the others calling to us from the world. This is not possible aside from spending time with him in study of His Word, in prayer, and in fellowship. You cannot get to know someone apart from time spent with them. You may know all the details about someone, but that is not the same as knowing them personally. How much more so with getting to know our Lord? The disciples knew Jesus up close and personal, and we can too.

How do we do this? It is very simple. Basically we spend time with Him.

1. We start reading our Bibles. It is God's word to His children, and He will explain to us what He requires, and we will learn what pleases Him. Then as we read it we learn to apply it to our lives. God's word does have the ability through the working of the Holy Spirit to change our lives (Rom 12:1–2). As we read and learn we also become more adept in learning to submit to His will by doing what the Bible says. Charles Swindoll says it is as we learn more about God that He will reveal Himself and provide all the motivation we need to follow Him into obedience and Christian service.[167]

2. As we study our Bibles and learn of Him we are spending time with Him and learning the sound of His voice. We are listening to Him. We are starting to confide in Him as we fellowship with Him. It is through prayer and Christian meditation that we accomplish this when we dwell on what His word says, turning

---

[167] Charles R. Swindoll and Roy B. Zuck, *Understanding Christian Theology*, 138.

it over in our minds. Reading it, studying it, and asking Him what it is that He is trying to relate to us. Mulling over this continually and then allowing the Holy Spirit to speak to us. He wants to teach us and is pleased when we want to know what He has to say. When we do this it brings us to basic communications 101, and it's called prayer. It is essential to our Christian walk.

We need to pray continually or be in a state of prayer where we are listening to hear what He is trying to teach us, always ready to pray when needed at the drop of a hat. It's simply a matter of always being in touch with Him and being prepared to pray. When we lift up the needs of others and bring their needs before the Father, we can seek forgiveness for our own sins. Then as we praise and worship Him we are led to lay our supplications before Him, knowing full well that He cares for us and will supply all of our needs (Phil 4:19). Basically we are spending time with Him getting to know Him. What a joy it is. Knowing God leads us to trust Him more, and this leads us to obedience.

Abraham provided us with a perfect example when he offered Isaac. He knew God intimately and obeyed God willingly. The order is significant. If you know someone and know his or her heart and where he or she is coming from, you are much more willing to obey them. If that person is wise and all powerful and loves you, and you know he or she would do nothing to harm you, then you will most likely obey that person because you have learned to trust them. Obedience motivated by love is the essential prerequisite to knowing God better.[168]

3. Then we need the fellowship of other believers. In Hebrews 10:25 we are told not to forsake the assembling of ourselves together. We are to find and be involved in a community of other believers. This is not optional; it is necessary for our Christian

---

[168] Charles R. Swindoll, Roy B. Zuck, 235.

growth (Heb 11:25). It is there we will be encouraged, while being held accountable for our actions and thoughts. It is there we will find acceptance and correction. It is there we will grow.

Christianity is not a spectator sport; we are the players. We are a team—a part of the body of Christ—and we need one another so that we can grow and mature in Christ collectively and individually. Fellowship with other believers is vital to our well-being as a Christian. There are no Lone Ranger Christians. We are all part of the body of Christ and need to do the part we were created for so that others might be encouraged and blessed by us as well.

If we do not take up the function God has for us in the body, then the body itself is hindered and unable to work at full capacity. We need one another whether that thought appeals to us or not. It is a blessed thing. It is only as the church comes together in unity of heart and mind centered on the person of Jesus Christ and His Word that we truly learn obedience. It can be a tough place to learn, but if we make the effort and give it our best, the blessings are beyond belief.

As we learn these disciplines we learn to walk in obedience according to the will of God and not our own will. Obedience is not multiple choice for the Christian.

God commands us to obey. It is not now nor ever has been a mere suggestion.

In Deuteronomy 27:10 God commanded the Israelites to listen, to pay attention, to understand, and to obey.

In Deuteronomy 30:8, again He commanded them to obey *all* of His commands. In 1 Samuel 15:22; Samuel tells us God has more delight in obedience than sacrifices. In, Jeremiah 7:22–23 the Lord again speaks of walking in obedience in all His commands.

In John 14:15, 21, 23, Jesus told His disciples that if we love Him we will keep His commands. In verse 24 it says that those who do not keep His commands do not love Him. Notice the change. In the Old Testament they were required to keep all the commands. This was a work-based salvation. Now, in the New Testament, our obedience is due to the fact that we love Him, being a natural response to our (already obtained) salvation as opposed to working for it.

Acts 5:29 tells us we should obey God rather than men. In Romans 6:16–18 Paul says we are servants to those we obey. Therefore, we can see that obedience is not just for the Old Testament but for New Testament believers as well.

Deuteronomy 28:2 says it is a condition of blessing to observe and do all the commandments.

Deuteronomy 28:15 sees judgment for those who do not observe and do all that He commanded.

Swindoll said: "Israel did not earn God's blessing through obedience. Rather their obedience simply maintained their covenant with God, who is the source of all blessing." In Ephesians 3:1, Christians are to obey God, not to get blessed but rather because they have already been blessed. Our obedience to Christ is an outward expression of our love and appreciation for all that He has done for us. John 14:15[169] Swindoll goes on to say that obedience is the "distinguishing characteristic" of those who belong to Christ.[170]

Peter Taylor Forsythe has some interesting thoughts on obedience as well, stating that neither man nor woman has any authority within himself or herself. The only authority we have is in Christ. Then it is only when we present Christ, His Word, and His church properly that we retain that authority. The authority we have as believers is effective as we represent that truth by walking faithfully in obedience. He goes on to say: "Faith is in its nature obedience." It's not so much a sympathy as it is a sympathetic obedience, yet always obedience—this attitude to the one who has a right over us regardless of His response to us. We are to trust and obey even in the midst of any disregard by Him or rebuff of His answer. "He is

---

[169] Charles R. Swindoll and Roy B. Zuck, 235.
[170] Ibid.

our God, not because he loves or pitied us, but because in his love and pity He redeemed us."[171]

Conclusion

Scripture tells us very plainly that we are saved by grace and grace alone. Yet with this beautiful grace so rich and free comes a responsibility on our part not to abuse it. Grace is a precious and priceless gift to be cherished and held in high esteem as the greatest of all treasures granted to man. Willem A. VanGerem has some interesting thoughts on this. He says that part of God's creating man in His own image involved man's responsibility. Adam and Eve were given responsibility in the garden, and they were to stay within the context of God's moral order (Gn 1:28, 2:2–3, 24; Eph 4:24). He points out that "because God endowed them with his image and with his grace, they were capable of keeping and enhancing the spiritual, moral, and social order." The test, as it were, was a test of Adam's love for the Father. Adam was not obedient and therefore proved his lack of trust and love for God.[172]

We can see then that our first responsibility is to obey God's word, completely and at any cost (Lk 14:26–33). We are to love nothing or no one more than God. We do not obey for selfish ends; rather it springs out of a love for God and others. Matthew 22:37–40 says:

> We are to love God with all of our heart soul and mind. This is His first command with the second being to love others as we love ourselves. It is upon

---

[171]   Peter Taylor Forsythe, *The Principals of Authority* (London: Haddor and Stoughton, 1912), 63–64.

[172]   Willem A. VanGemeren, *Five Views on the Law and the Gospel* (Grand Rapids, MI: Zondervan Publishing House, 1996), chap. 1, p. 18.

these two laws that all the law and the prophets hang upon.

John 14:21 says: "If we love Him we will keep his commands."[173] According to Swindoll and Zuck, there are basically four principles to biblical obedience, and they are:

1. Obedience to God's word is emphasized in both Old and New Testaments. Exodus 19:5–6 said if the children of Israel would obey His voice He promised Israel would be a holy nation unto Him. Whereas in Matthew 28:20, Jesus instructed that they teach believers to observe all things whatsoever He commanded them, and then He would be with them always. In Luke 8:21, Jesus stated that His family were those who hear the word of God and do it. James 1:22 tells us Jesus wants us to be not just hearers of the word, but doers. The New Testament uses verbs such as obey, do, observe, and keep in relation to the word of God.

2. In order to obey, we first need to know what to obey. John 13:17 tells us that if we know these things, happy are we if we do them. We must have biblical truth before we can practice it. In John 14:21, Jesus says that he that hath my commandments, and keeps them, he it is that loves me.

Once we learn it we must practice it. Failure to practice known biblical truth is sin. James 4:17 says: "To him that knows to do good and doesn't do it, to him it is sin." When we disobey there are serious consequences (Acts 5:1–11). Who can forget Ananias and Sapphira, who conspired to deceive the apostles? In James 1:22–25, we are told to be doers of the word, and not hearers only, thereby deceiving ourselves.

---

[173] Charles Swindoll, Roy B. Zuck, 1021.

3. Obeying brings God's blessing (Jn 13:17). "If ye know these things, happy are ye if ye do them." Luke 11:28 tells us, "Blessed are they that hear the word of God, and keep it." There are special blessings for obedience.

4. To effectively obey scriptures we must reject sin (Jas 1:21), forsake sin, and break free from all sin at regeneration.[174]

Joe Dallas thinks: "To steward truth properly, we need first to know it, live in conformity to it, and then express it" (1 Tm 4:26, 2 Tm 3:16–17). "When we know and live in conformity to the truth, we will then be able to teach, being patient and meek with those who oppose the truth. Trusting that God will give them repentance to the acknowledging of the truth" (2 Tm 2:25.)[175]

One cannot help but wonder, what if Abraham had not obeyed God? Because he believed and obeyed, it was accounted to him as righteousness (Jas 2:23; Gn 15:6). Abraham was known as the father of faith because he was faithful. Noah listened and obeyed, and mankind was saved as a result, as well as the animal kingdom. What if Moses had decided he didn't want to do what God was asking, preferring to stay and raise sheep instead? Who then would have delivered Israel from bondage? What if Jesus had not been obedient? Philippians 2:8 says: "Jesus, being found in fashion as a man, he humbled himself, and became obedient unto death, even the death of the cross."

The New Testament places a lot of emphasis on the obedience of Jesus. Why? It is because "Jesus's obedience stands in stark contrast to Adam's disobedience."[176] Romans 5:12–21 (KJV) explains how one man, Adam, through his disobedience brought death and sin

---

[174] Charles R. and Swindoll, Roy B. Zuck, 1021.

[175] Joe Dallas, *Now What? Same Sex Marriage and Today's Church*. Article ID: JAF6371. CRI.

[176] Gary Hardin, "Obedience:" *Holman Illustrated Bible Dictionary, ed.* (Nashville, TN: Holman Bible Publishers, 2003), 1206.

to the world. It says "through the offense of one many died. (v. 15). How much more the gift of grace, by one man, Jesus Christ, many live. Jesus's motivation was a strong desire to obey the will of God (Lk 4:43, Jn 5:30). By living a life of obedience, Jesus proved Himself to be the savior (Heb 5:7–10). Even His death on the cross was considered a sacrifice of obedience (Rom 5:19, Heb 10:7–10).[177] If Jesus had not been obedient, we would all still be lost in our sin.

Obedience is something we as Christians really need to take into consideration because it is important. A disobedient life is an offense to God and a very bad witness to those around us. All one has to do is take a look at Adam and see what destruction his noncompliance caused. If that isn't enough, take a long look at Samson (Jgs 14–18). It could be argued that he eventually did God's will in destroying God's enemies; however, that was only as a last resort of a wasted, sinful life. Imagine what He might have accomplished had he walked in obedience. We have no idea what God may do in our lives if we will just walk in compliance to His word.

Grudem explains it like this: "There are many motives for obedience. Yet, for the Christian obedience to God and faithfulness to Him in every circumstance is far more important than this mortal life" (Acts 21:13, 25:11, 20:24; Rv 12:11).[178]

Let's look at some motives for obedience that we might consider.

1. A strong desire to please God (Jn 14:15, 21).
2. So that we may have a clear mind and conscience (Rom 13:5, 2 Tim 1:3, 1 Pt 3:16).
3. So that we may be more effective in our witness (2 Tim 2:20–21).
4. To win others to Jesus (1 Pt 3:9–12).

[177] Gary Hardin, "Obedience:" *Holman Illustrated Bible Dictionary*, ed., 1206.
[178] *Wayne Grudem, Bible Doctrine: Essential Teaching of the Christian Faith* (Grand Rapids, MI: Zondervan, 1999), 350.

5. That we might receive God's blessing in our lives and ministries, (1 Pt 3:9–12).

6. In order to avoid God's displeasure and discipline, "the fear of the Lord" (Acts 5:11, 9:31; 2 Cor 5:11, 7:1; Eph 4:30).

7. To receive heavenly rewards (Mt 6:19–21; Lk 19:14–19; 1 Cor 3:12–15, 5:9–10).

8. To cultivate a deeper walk with God (Mt 5:8; Jn 14:21; 1 Jn 1:6, 3:21–22).

9. To think that angels would glorify God for our obedience (1 Tim 5:21, 1 Pt 1:12).

10. That we might have peace in our lives (Phil 4:19).

11. To be filled with joy (Heb 12:1–2).

12. The desire to do what God commands for no other reason than they are right (Phil 4:8, Ps 40:8, 1 Jn 2:4–6).[179]

We can ascertain that: (1) God commands us to obey, (2) there are four basic principles to obedience, and (3) we have strong motives for obedience. The question is why are we dragging out feet? There are blessings galore in heaven and on earth for those who walk in obedience —blessings that are far beyond anything we can imagine here on earth (1 Cor 2:9). Again we are not obedient in order to be blessed of God; we are already blessed by what God did at Calvary. Rather we are obedient because we love Him, and we love others. The blessings are simply a by-product of that obedience.

There must be a reckoning of ourselves to have died unto sin and been resurrected to newness of life in Christ Jesus. Then we can give our *all* to the Holy Spirit. Then we practice whatever self-discipline is necessary to walk in His Spirit, trampling under our feet all lust of the flesh. Towzer would go on to say that God, who gave all to us on Calvary, will continue to give all to and through us as we strive to know Him more intimately.[180]

---

[179] Grudem, 350.

[180] A. W. Tozer, *The Knowledge of the Holy: The Attributes of God* (Harper Collins, 1897–1963), 116.

Who can forget the words of that beautiful old hymn "Trust and Obey"? Just reading those words as they are so eloquently arranged in song by John H. Sammis (1846–1919).

Psalm 37:3–5 (KJV) tells us to "commit thy way unto the Lord; trust also in him; and he shall bring it to pass." Then in John 8:31 (KJV): "If ye continue in my word then are ye my disciples indeed." Again in 14:23 (KJV): "If a man loves me, he will keep my word." James warns us in 2:14–26 about faith without works. Then John, in 1 John 2:6 (KJV) tells us: "He that saith he abideth in him ought himself also so to walk, even as he walked."

While it is true that salvation is God's responsibility, it is also true that our responsibility is to trust in that salvation and then to obey its truths. We can experience the abiding presence of Christ as we make up our minds to trust Him completely and then obey His leadings in everything we do.

Let us determine in our hearts and minds and spirits to become acquainted with God and His word, so that we may come to recognize His voice that we might be able to not just call Him Lord and Savior, but friend as well (Jn 15:14–15). In so doing, learn to become obedient in all that we say and do, so that on that day we will hear those most beautiful of words: "Well done, thou good and faithful servant."

Chuck Swindoll would close it like this: "We have discovered that to be a friend of God is one who knows Him intimately and obeys Him willingly. A friend of God is characterized by uncompromising obedience to Christ and a growing knowledge of Christ." [181] The same could be called a true disciple of Christ.

---

[181]   Charles Swindoll, Roy B. Zuck, 237.

6

CHAPTER

Holiness and Grace

To understand true holiness and the need thereof, we must first understand God's grace. Having taken a good look at obedience and the necessity of it in the Christian life, we need to ask ourselves if there is a duty afforded to us by this grace. If so, what is it? This is not for our salvation, as that has already been established for us in Christ. Shedd put it like this: "Holiness is where the believer begins to co-operate with God the Spirit through the process of sanctification. Sanctification being both a grace and a duty."[182] In Romans 12:1–2, Paul even goes so far as to say this is our "reasonable duty." It is the least we can do in light of all that Christ has done for us. This can only come about from a deep love, inspired by the mercy and grace of God, through Jesus Christ (Lk 1:68–75, Rom 8:15, 2 Cor 5:14, 1 Jn 4:18).[183] Let's take a look at

---

[182] William T. Shedd, *Dogmatic Theology,* 3rd ed. (Phillipsburg, NJ: P&R Publishing, 2003), 804.

[183] Bryan Chapell, *Holiness by Grace: Delighting in the Joy That Is Our Strength* (Wheaton, IL: Crossway, 2001).

grace and how it relates to holiness. Is there a connecting thread, and if so what is it?

There is no means by which we can fully comprehend the full span of God's grace. It is so wide and deep and rich that we can merely skim the surface. Grace was not something new that just sprang up in the New Testament. It has been there from the beginning all the way back to the garden. It was grace that God showered on Adam and Eve after the fall (Gn 3:21). That same grace that was shown to Cain after murdering Abel (Gn 4:18) was also shown to Noah and his family during the flood (Gn 6:8–22), and then to Abraham and the nation of Israel (Gn 12:1–3). The Israelites continued as a nation to reject God, proving once again that they were deserving of the same punishment as the pagan nations surrounding them. Still, God's mercies were upon them, and His grace abounded to them. The list could go on and on as to how His mercy and grace were extended to the nation of Israel throughout the Old Testament. We can see that grace is not something new or surprising. It is just God's nature to be gracious and merciful. The exemplification of this was seen in Jesus (Col 1:13–20). Even the giving of the law on Mount Sinai was God's grace to Israel, so that the Israelite might carry their religious beliefs over into their everyday affairs of life,[184] affecting and blessing the rest of the world through God's grace.

It is this same grace that would led Martin Luther to proclaim during a time of deep meditation that "he who through faith is righteous shall live. There I began to understand that the righteousness of God is that by which the righteous lives by a gift of God, namely by faith … Here I felt that I was altogether born again and had entered paradise itself through open gates."[185]

Along about here somewhere we should be starting to hear the hounds baying in the background. Aren't we saved by grace and not

---

[184]   John Williams Drane, *Introducing the New Testament,* completely revised and updated (Oxford: Lion Publishing, 2,000), 410.

[185]   F. F. Bruce, *The Epistle to the Hebrews,* revised ed. (Grand Rapids, Eerdmens, 1990), 138.

by works? Failing to realize that faith builds trust and that trust leads to obedience. Although it is true that we are saved by faith through God's grace, it is also true that we have become a new creation with a new nature in Christ (2 Cor 5:17). We no longer live as slaves to our old sinful ways and habits that characterized our old lives (Eph 2:1). We have been changed, not by our own effort, but by God's glorious grace. It is not a change we can make on our own (Gal 6:15). Once again that change is a result of God's grace on our behalf.[186] "We have been delivered from the power of darkness and translated, by God into the kingdom of His dear Son" (Col 1:13). It is a work that begins on the inside and works its way out.

God changes our hearts through His grace and the power of His Holy Spirit. It is a supernatural work of the Holy Spirit in our lives. As one writer would explain it, salvation is a good and perfect gift from God. He was the one who came up with the plan to make reconciliation possible, and He is the one who keeps us. None of us deserve to have our sins forgiven. Nor does walking in that forgiveness constitute a "work." When all is said and done, it is God who provides the righteousness required to demonstrate that restored fellowship between God and man. The ability to walk in that righteousness is grace, also.[187] This too is the good news of the gospel. Our utter dependence is upon Christ. Even to live daily for Him requires His grace.

The grace that saved us does not end at Calvary. For the Christian, Calvary is where it all begins. What a magnificent grace this is. We do not want to sell it short. This same grace that saves us will also keep us and deliver us to the throne one day in good standing (1 Jn 3:2–3). It is a saving grace and not just a past experience, according

---

[186] Thomas Oden, *Classic Christianity: A Systematic Theology* (Harper Collins, 1992), 606.

[187] Mark R. Quanstrom, *From Grace to Grace* (Kansas City: Beacon Hill, 2011), 63.

to Quanstrom.[188] His grace leads us and sustains us in our walk; it uplifts us.

Shedd said that "sanctification is (receiving the growth enabling completing, maturing, perfecting grace of God that leads toward holiness of heart and life)."[189] God, in His great plan of salvation, also made the provision for us to be able to live for Him (Heb 10:10). According to Jones, "God, is the 'Agent'of this work of holiness within the believer. That first move, the motive, the force, all is the power of God by His grace working is us, both to will and to do."[190] Where the apostle Paul said God's grace was sufficient for every circumstance in his life (2 Cor 12:9).

In Acts 2 we read that God poured out His Holy Spirit to all believers on the day of Pentecost. He is still pouring out His Spirit on all believers today. This too was another great work of grace on God's part. Keeping God's grace in sight let us search the scripture to see what it has to say about grace and its relationship with holiness.

Many would contend that holiness is legalism or salvation by works, but is this true? The desire to be holy as God is holy should be in every Christian's heart. If we are not being sanctified and living a holy life then there is a serious question regarding our salvation experience. God's word commands us to "Be Holy as He is Holy (1 Pt 1:13–21). The desire to live a holy life should originate from the great salvation we have experienced and in light of the holiness of God.[191] We are, after all, called to be a holy priesthood (1 Pt 2:9).

Are God's grace and the believer's holiness diametrically opposed? Can holiness for the believer and God's grace be uttered in the same sentence without controversy? Or is there a link between the two that we cannot see, and if so, what might that link be?

---

[188] Dr. Michael Brown, *Hypergrace*, Kindle, location 2022.

[189] Shedd, 607.

[190] D. M. Lloyd-Jones, *God the Holy Spirit* (Wheaton, IL: Crossway Books, 1997), 203–209.

[191] Michael L. Brown, *Hypergrace* (Kindle location 202).

While holiness is something every born-again believer should seek after, we need to remember that without God's grace there can be no holiness. Sanctification is also one of God's graces bestowed on Christians at their conversion. This sanctification, which begins at justification, is received by faith. Sanctification or holiness is God's grace every bit as much as our forgiveness from sins."[192] Oden points out that this is "Sanctifying Grace." It is just as important to the believer as is "Saving or Justifying Grace,"[193] and is part and parcel with it.

Sanctification leads us into God's path to follow Him. We can rest assured that God's grace operating through the Holy Spirit will never lead us into sin but rather will lead us toward holiness and good works (Eph 2:8–10; Jas 1:25). Luther said, "Faith is known by its works just like a tree is known by its fruit."[194] It isn't so much the faith that pleases God as it is the trust that faith instills and the obedience that trust produces. All of which is a result of faith in God's grace. According to James 2:18–24, the works or obedience are just proof of our faith.

Even in seeking to live in holiness we are still dependent on God's grace and not through our own efforts. This too is God's grace. There is nothing here for a Christian to lay claim to or boast about (Eph 2:8–10). Just simply the cross of Christ, Lloyd-Jones says this, sanctification or the process of sanctification begins the moment we have placed our faith (trust) in Christ. At that moment of being born again, or regenerated, something has entered into us that will separate us from sin.[195]

This is God's grace at work in the believer too.

Wesley said that "when we find those old things reemerging, it is a reminder that the carnal nature has not been wholly destroyed."[196]

---

[192] Quanstrom, 64.

[193] Oden, 611.

[194] Luther, *The Freedom of a Christian*, MLS:71–801.

[195] Lloyd-Jones, 203–9.

[196] John Wesley, WJW 5:223–33.

Then he goes on to remind us that "even though sin may remain in the believer, it no longer reigns in those who have received justifying grace."[197]

Hodges would remind us that we are not talking perfection; we are speaking of progress in the Christian walk. No one is perfect except God. But again, God's grace is leading us into and through a sanctification process from the moment we become saved. This sanctifying work is to apply the work of Christ to the heart and life of a believer. It is an experiential process beginning with a new birth.[198] Through the guidance of the Holy Spirit we are being purified and made into the image of Christ more and more each day (1 Jn 3:3). Campbell would make note of another wonder of God's grace in that He has now written His laws upon our hearts (Jer 31:33; Heb 8:10, 10:16).[199] Every time we decide to do right rather than wrong, it is God's Spirit and grace at work in us. Each time we put away our desire in favor of someone else's need, we see God's grace at work. When we love that person that is so unlovable, it is God's grace enabling us by the Holy Spirit.

When a Christian really begins to understand all that God has wrought in the heart of a believer and the limitless grace at his or her disposal, that person cannot help but follow the leading of the Spirit, which always leads one to holiness.

Christians Are Called to Walk in the Spirit Rather Than in the Flesh

We are living in a world of increasing violence, hostility, and lawlessness, with much of that hostility directed toward Christians.

---

197   John Wesley, WJW 5:144–46.

198   Charles Hodges, *Systematic Theology*, vol. 3 (Peabody, MA: Hendrickson: 2008).

199   Ian D. Campbell, *Opening Up Exodus: Opening Up Commentary* (Leominster: Day One Publications, 2006), 83.

According to Oz Guiness, it seems that our worldview today is what he calls ABC, meaning that people are accepting "anything besides Christ."[200] With attacks from the left and the religious cults on the right, Christianity is being ridiculed, mocked, and held up to public scorn. In many places around the world Christians are being slaughtered just because they claim the name of Christ. Even in America we are seeing these things beginning to happen, where even our churches are no longer safe.

As a result of this, Christians have a challenge ahead. This is a new concept for many American Christians today. That challenge is not only to live lives acceptable and pleasing to God, [201] but to shine forth in a world that seems to be succumbing to darkness all around. The Bible says that "when the enemy comes in like a flood, God said that the Spirit will lift up a standard against it" (Is 59:19 KJV). Could that standard be holiness?

As a result of all these things, it appears that many of our leaders today are leaning toward the doctrine of antinomianism, referring to this doctrine as "the New Reformation" or "a Gospel of Radical Grace," teaching that they have discovered something far beyond what Luther rediscovered in the reformation period and taking grace to an unprecedented level.

At the same time, we need to be very careful not to minimize grace. We can never begin to understand the immensity of God's grace nor the scope that it encompasses. Instead, we need to ask the question did grace end at Calvary? Or is that grace still actively at work in the lives of believers? As Christians struggle each day to live for Christ, they can take heart knowing God has graciously bestowed them with His Holy Spirit. When we take the time to consider it, even the giving of the Holy Spirit on the day of Pentecost itself was a wonderful provision of God's grace to believers.

---

[200]   Oz Guiness, *Impossible People* (Downers Grove: Intervarsity Press, 2016).
[201]   R. C. Sproul, *Following Christ* (Wheaton, IL: Tyndale House, 1996).

Calvin, that great champion of grace and faith, still taught that sanctification was a progressive as well as positional process. He states: "Our whole lives as Christians should be one of aspiration after piety Seeing we are called to holiness" (Eph I 4:1, Thes, iv, 5).[202]

There are three aspects of this process called sanctification or holiness or piety.

1. Positional. This is the part that takes place at conversion where we "have been" sanctified (past tense) and where Christ's righteousness has been imputed to us, and we have been made holy and our sins forgiven. This is by God alone through grace.
2. Experiential. First Peter 1:6 says that this is the "now" of salvation as in (present tense) where the Holy Spirit is sanctifying us, and we are in the process of being made holy. God is still the active leader and director of this phase of grace. Christians also have an active role.
3. Future or culmination. This is where we "will be" fully sanctified (future tense) (1 Jn 3:1–3, Eph 5:26–27, Jude 23–25).

We can see from this illustration that we can safely say that we have been sanctified, we are being sanctified, and we will one day be sanctified fully,[203] showing us that being made holy is a work in progress for the Christian.

Christians have been called to holiness, and the only way we can do this is through God's grace of sanctifying power. It is interesting that even Calvin and Wesley agreed upon this point. Hoekema said, "Calvin also agreed with Wesley that holy living was the goal of Salvation."[204]

---

202 John Calvin, *Institutes of the Christian Religion,* II, 3.6.5., p. 5.
203 Charles Caldwell Ryrie, *A Survey of Bible Doctrine* (Chicago: Moody Press, 1995).
204 Anthony Hoekema, "A Response to Dieter," in *Five Views of Sanctification* (Grand Rapids, MI: Zondervan, 1987).

Conclusion

The question is this: What relationship does grace have with holiness? Well, pretty much everything. It is a beautiful working relationship brought about by God's wonderful mercy and grace, put into action by the Holy Spirit. When you divorce one from the other, you weaken and even in some cases destroy the basic structure.

This bond between grace and holiness is one of complete beauty and harmony.

Grace and holiness are not enemies but closely linked friends, working together to shape each blood-washed person into the image of Jesus. This process begins at the new birth and continues on until our lives are completed, at which point we will enter into the presence of Jesus.

We are accepted into the kingdom by God's grace, and we are ushered into the presence of Jesus by God's grace. So ultimately it is all by grace. Better yet, it is grace upon grace. Even so, it is grace that moves us forward into holiness. This same grace gives us freedom from sin and delivers us throughout our lives. Without this marvelous grace moving and working in our lives every day we would be unable to continue. We would be helpless and defeated. But God did not leave us here to battle alone without the necessary resources. He made provision for us to be victorious and to live our lives in a manner to glorify Him by giving us His Holy Spirit. Praise to His name.

We are going to move on to take a closer look at how grace operates through the law and the gospel.

The Gospel and the Law: Compatible or Combative?

O n the subject of holiness we cannot overlook the law and how it might affect us in our Christian walk today.

If there is an active relationship between the law and the gospel, then what type of relationship are we talking about? Is it one of antagonism or harmony? Are they friends or foes? When looking into the law, the Christian faces two great pitfalls. The first is legalism. This is where a person tries to earn their salvation (justification) from works as opposed to faith in the finished work of Christ. The second equally dangerous is to completely dismiss the importance of the law. This leads to licentious behavior or antinomianism. We know that somewhere between these two extremes we should find the truth. We will be studying these two more closely in following chapters. Before we do this we want to see what type of a connection exists, if one does, between the law and the gospel in order to develop a deeper appreciation of how this affects the daily life of a believer.

Stephenson says: "In Christ the Christian now has a new relationship to the law and a new standard of obedience."[205] Some would strongly disagree, arguing that the law has been done away with and therefore has nothing to do with the Christian today. Is this true, just because we are now under the covenant of grace? Herschel is quite adamant that law and grace are totally incompatible, claiming that one negates the other. He points out that it can be likened to a fork in the road where the law ends and grace begins—a distinct point where one is forced to choose between the two. He makes note that one cannot go down both ways. With the death and resurrection of Jesus he claims we leave the road of the law and turn onto the fork of grace, thereby passing from the one (law) and clinging closely to the other (grace). Although there is truth here, there is also some confusion. He goes on to say that you cannot have both, as it is one or the other. "If you follow the law road then you do not have grace and are cut off from it. If it is the grace road you follow then it is a gift and cannot be the law. If it is a gift by grace, then it cannot be the law."[206] As a result it would appear as though the two are completely incompatible. Still, we need to ask ourselves are they?

Scripture confirms that our justification is by grace alone and then our salvation is a "gift." Does this necessarily mean that we are to utterly forsake God's law? Is there any value to the Christian in the law? Stephenson would disagree with the fork in the road analogy by saying, "Where most would agree that Grace and the Law are not the same that is not a reason to believe that they are in conflict."[207]

[205] Lester L. Stephenson, *A Biblicist View of the Law and Gospel* (Greenville, SC: Ambassador Int., 2017), Kindle ed.

[206] Herschel H. Hobbs, *My Favorite Illustrations* (Nashville, TN: Broadman Press, 1990), 131–32.

[207] Stephenson, chap. 10.

We know that we are saved (justified) completely by grace, it being the free gift of God. No problem here, but does this mean that when we enter into the grace of our Lord we throw the law away? We need to ask ourselves this: Did the law die? Is it dead? Gladly, no. It is alive and well in the heart of every born-again believer (Rom 3:13–15).

If there is a bond between the gospel and the law, it is sadly being overlooked in our churches today, which leads us to the question of if there is a link, what exactly is it? Jesus said He came to fulfill the law; He did not say He came to do away with or destroy it as some claim (Mt 5:17–19).

When speaking of following the law, Jesus's death and resurrection fulfilled the laws dealing with the Jewish ceremonial, sacrificial, judicial, civil, and dietary laws. Yet, here we are left with the moral laws—those moral laws having to do with how we relate to God and others. Those are the very laws, decrees, precepts, or commands that would teach us how we are to conduct our lives on a daily basis. What are we to do with these?

Wiersbe seems to think it is quite interesting that nine of the ten commandments are repeated in the New Testament as well as the Epistles, which would render them still effective today—meaning that we then are still subject to them as Christians. They haven't changed with the exception of the commandment concerning the Sabbath, as that one belonged to the nation of Israel for a particular time and place. As a result it does not have the same meaning for the Christian today as it did to the Jews then (Rom 14:1–9).[208]

By reading and becoming familiar with the Old Testament as well as the New Testament we learn about God's character. As children of God, we need to get serious about sin and living a holy life. Odin suggests that when we are born again by faith in Christ that new birth brings along a birth of a new spiritual nature. This

---

[208] Warren B. Wiersbe, *The Bible Exposition Commentary* (Wheaton, IL:Victor Books, 1996), 1 Peter 1:16–17.

new nature has a bold resistance to sin and will not ever again tolerate its existence in a believer.[209] God is still a holy and a righteous father (Jn 17:11, 25). He has not changed. One of His attributes is His immutability (Heb 13:8, Jn 8:28). He does not compromise with sin. He is merciful and gracious to those who call upon His name for salvation, freely forgiving them when they do (Acts 2:21). As Christians we have nothing to fear from the law, as the law does not take anything away from grace; it merely enhances it.

We still need to keep in mind that God disciplines those He loves, and there can be severe consequences if we disobey His word. He will not permit His children to continue to live in sin. Jesus came to eradicate sin (Mt 1:21, 1 Tm 1:15), not the law. If we are truly His children then we should reflect His nature.[210]

How then, are we to reconcile the two? Can they even be reconciled? Jesus said repeatedly that if we love Him we will keep His commands. What commands was He speaking of (Mt 28:19 20; John 14:15, 21–24)?

Are the law and gospel diametrically opposed? Or were they meant to balance one another by working together in harmony like a countermelody in a symphony? Where the law was once in the forefront taking the lead, now grace has superseded by taking the forefront with the countermelody (of the law) supportive in the background. If the law was the foundation on which grace was brought to us, then is it so hard to believe that this law is still good for the soul of the believer? Are Christians no longer expected to follow the Golden Rule, spoken of by Jesus (Mt 7:12)?

Was God's grace not dispersed freely while actively working throughout the Old Testament? Maybe in a different form than we know it today, but grace nonetheless. Or was God's grace reserved only for those under the New Testament? To be sure, God's salvific grace was for those under the new covenant, but God's grace has

---

[209]   Odin, 606.

[210]   Wiersbe, 1 Pt 1:16–17.

been at work since Eden. Does it not then stand to reason that those who are called by His name would be walking in conformity to God's law today?

God has called His children to holiness (1 Pt 1:15). Knowing this then, is it so hard to believe that He would be the one who enables us to walk in obedience? Isn't this the purpose of the Holy Spirit—to lead us and guide us into God's truth? Doesn't the Holy Spirit always lead us toward holiness? We know He never leads us toward sin.

Where do we learn what holiness is? In the early days it was from the Old Testament and the laws of God. Today is no different except now God has given us new hearts and a new spirit. He even went so far as to actually write those same laws upon our hearts (Ez 36:26, Jer 31:33). It is from the law that we learn discernment and discover right from wrong? We ask again, is it possible to live a life that is pleasing to God? Is it wrong for a Christian to want to do this? Are the commands given by Jesus in John 14:15, 21, 23–24 different in nature than those moral laws given by Moses? Bashan reveals that "laws written on clay tablets" could never save; they were there to convict of sin. Under the New Covenant, however, the Holy Spirit wrote those laws upon our hearts. They according to Bashan "communicate life and righteousness," while supplying us with the power to obey God's commandments (Jer 31:33; Ez 11:19–20; Rom 7:12–16, 8:4; 2 Cor 3:3, 6–9; Heb 10:14, 13:20–21).[211]

In Galatians 5:13–15 Paul reminds the Galatians that they were called to freedom from:

- sin,
- guilt,
- fear,
- and from trying to be good enough.

---

[211]   Greg L. Bahnsen, *The Theonomic Reformed Approach to Law and Gospel: Five Views of Law and Gospel* (Grand Rapids, MI: Zondervan, 1996), 102.

Some may have abused this freedom by indulging themselves and by believing God approves of their continuing to live in sin and has already forgiven them from future sins. Paul states that Christian freedom is not permission to do wrong but the liberty to do right. Real freedom displays itself in love and service to others.

Loving others was always the aim of the Jewish law (but was impossible to do). Therefore, Jesus died to fulfill that law (which was impossible for us). Through the power of His resurrection and the help of the Holy Spirit we also can do impossible things. Through Christ we can do all things (Phil 4:13). What once was impossible for man has become possible through faith in Christ. His death and resurrection set us free from the burden of keeping the law and from death and sin. As a result we are free not to keep on breaking the law but free to keep it. Now, thanks to Jesus fulfilling the law, we can at last obey it in the proper way and for the proper reasons.[212]

Did the coming of the gospel wipe out the law? Let's investigate a little further and see. Always we must return to the word of God. What does it say? It doesn't matter what anyone else says; the Bible is our rule and guide. Is it erroneous to think that just because we are under grace that the law has no influence in our lives any longer? Paul stated very clearly in Romans 3:31: "Do we then make void the law through faith? God forbid: yea, we establish the law." Then in chapter 7 of Romans, while talking about the law and how it showed him his sin, he stated in verse 12: "Wherefore the law is holy, and the commandment holy, and just and good."

Jesus often used the term "It is written." Why? Because it carries great authority for the believer. Wiersbe points out that Jesus used the Word of God to defeat Satan (Mt 4:1–11, Eph 6:17). The scriptures are still beneficial to us, as a light to guide us in a dark world (Ps 119:105, 2 Pt 1:19). It is the Word of God that strengthens us (Mt 4:1–10, 1 Pt 2:2). It is water to wash and cleanse us (Eph 5:25–27).

---

[212] Andrew Knowles, *The Bible Guide,* first Augsburg Books ed. (Minneapolis, MN: Augsburg, 2001), 610–11.

This same Word of God sanctifies us (Jn 17:17). If we delight in God's Word, meditate on it, and seek to obey it we will experience God's direction and blessing in our lives (Ps 1:1–3). The Word is where we go to learn more, so that we might come to know God better. To try and understand how His mind works that we might know or learn more of His will for our lives. The Word of God is how we learn to love Him and His Word and "as a result to live it," in order that we might have our minds and hearts transformed by that Word (Rom 12:1–2).[213]

Every Christian should be a student of the Old Testament. There is so much to be gleaned from it. It is through the Old Testament that we really start to understand the New Testament. Paul says in 2 Timothy 3:16: "ALL scripture is given by inspiration of God and profitable for teaching, for reproof, for correction and for training in righteousness." It is interesting that the scripture of which he was speaking of here was the Old Testament. Yes, we need to be very careful how we handle many Old Testament passages. Campbell stresses that we must be careful to interpret them in light of other scriptures.[214] As we do this we begin to see the truth and eternal principles set down by God through His law, not to mention we discover the beauty of that law.

When Jesus talks of the word we have to ask ourselves what "word" is He referring to? The only word they had at that time was our Old Testament. The same one Jesus taught from, as did all of the apostles, Paul, and the early church fathers. These scriptures are still valid for Christians today. God hasn't changed His mind. The difference now is that Jesus's death and resurrection make what was once impossible now possible.

Wiersbe tells us: "If we are willing to obey God, He will show us His truth (Jn 7:17). While God's methods of working may change from age to age, His character remains the same as do His spiritual

---

213 Wiersbe.
214 Ian D. Campbell, 83.

principles." [215] He is immutable—never changing. It is remarkable that God is the one who is steadfast, sure, and trustworthy due to His unchangeableness. Whereas man is the one who is fickle and capricious. We need to get our priorities straight. How do we do this? Jesus said, "by seeking first His kingdom and His righteousness, then all of these things will be added (Mt 6:33).

According to Knowles, in scripture nothing is lifted above the saving work that was accomplished on Calvary, including the law.[216] Our salvation is secured in Christ as is our righteousness. In Galatians 5, Paul explained that the Jewish Christians wanted the Gentiles to be circumcised because, as Knowles indicates, "the Jews assumed that the law was more important than the promise," believing the only way their faith could be expressed was by following the law.[217]

Paul's view was completely different. He believed and preached that all the conditions of the law were met by Christ. Now the purpose of God's righteousness was obvious. It was free for all who would put their faith in Christ to save them.[218] When we keep His commands we are doing it out of love and adoration as opposed to fear and condemnation. We do it simply because we have a new heart that wants to please God, not because we have to. Nor do we try to keep the letter of the law. What we do is walk in light of what we know of scripture as the Holy Spirit reveals it to us. Sinclair Ferguson said, "Persons who understand grace loves the law."[219]

Keith chimed in with the thought that "our salvation was settled at Calvary. However, we still have to deal with sin on a daily basis." Only by walking in the Spirit which is merely done by obedience and submitting to God's word and the leading of the Holy Spirit.

---

[215] Wiersbe.

[216] Andrew Knowles, *The Bible Guide:* 1st Augsburg books ed. (Minneapolis, MN: Augsburg, 2001), 608–9.

[217] Ibid.

[218] Ibid.

[219] Sinclair Ferguson, *"Law"* (Table Talk: Legionaires, 2016).

This is the only means by which believers can bear the fruit of the Spirit (Mt 7:17, Lk 6:43–44).[220]

From this we can see that maybe our perception of the gospel and the law needs a little adjustment. The law and the gospel message are not only compatible but harmonious. They work in conjunction with one another. As Kaiser asks: "Is the law opposed to the promises of God? Absolutely not (Rom 3:21)."[221] Knowles would tell us, "any solution that quickly runs the law out of town certainly cannot look to the Scriptures for any kind of comfort or support."[222]

Jesus has much to say about keeping God's commands. First, He said we are to love God with all our hearts and minds and souls. This encompasses the first four of the ten. Then the second, He said, was like the first in that we should love our neighbors as we love ourselves. This encompasses the other six. Jesus said, "On these two commandments hang all the law and the prophets" (Mt 22:40). When we truly love God we will have no graven images or other gods before Him. We won't take His name in vain or bring reproach upon His name by an ungodly life. We will honor our mothers and fathers. When we love our neighbors we will not harm them by stealing from them, killing them, bearing false witness against them, or covet their possessions. We will look out for them just the same as we would ourselves.

When people try to say that we are no longer under the law, this is misleading if not outright false. Jesus gave us two commandments in their place, but in so doing these two comprise the ten. As Campbell so aptly explains, we should always keep in mind that all of these commands reveal "God's moral authority and as such His moral authority which are the moral absolutes that govern and

[220] Keith Brooks, *Summarized Bible: Complete Summary of the New Testament* (Bellingham, WA: Logos Bible Software, 2009), 58.

[221] Walter C. Kaiser Jr., *As God's Gracious Guidance for the Promotion of Holiness: Five Views on Law and Gospel* (Grand Rapids, MI: Zonervan, 1996), 178.

[222] Knowles.

modify all of our behavior." Let's take a look at these commands; we know them well.

- Do not have any other god but me.
- Do not worship me in any way other than the way I prescribe.
- Do not use my name lightly.
- Keep my day holy.
- Honor your parents.
- Do not kill.
- Do not commit adultery.
- Do not steal.
- Do not tell lies.
- Do not covet.

It is obvious that these do, or should, govern all of our lives. They regulate not only the religious, but the personal, social, and political areas of our lives. They explain how we should live in relation to God and to one another. The order is significant because "true morality is founded in reverence to God."[223]

While many might argue this point, we need to keep in mind that Jesus took it one step further, when He said that even if a man looks upon a woman with lust he is guilty of adultery. Now it was no longer just the acts that were unacceptable and reproachable but the thoughts themselves, motivating us to walk in the Spirit rather than the flesh (Gal 5:16, 25).

The weaver is one illustration. If a person takes yarn or thread he or she can knit or crochet many beautiful one-of-a-kind creations. But they are using one thread only. It cannot be cut, as it will totally fall apart. If you pull on that thread, the whole piece will unravel. This can be very disheartening to the creator of the piece.

On the other hand if that same thread is woven together with another thread it is very durable. Why? Because it is bound together

---

[223] Ian D. Campbell, 83–85.

by at least two different threads in opposing directions, known as the weft and woof. It has strength and durability not available with knitted or crocheted pieces. It can be cut and sewn together to form garments, tents, fishing nets, etc. They used to weave sails for sailing ships in this manner due to its strength and durability.

The veil in the temple that was torn at Jesus's crucifixion was a woven item. Weaving is very sturdy and is still a very big part of our culture and economics around the world, as most of our clothing and textiles we use on a daily basis are made from woven material. Beautiful tapestries from antiquity still exist today because of their structural integrity.[224]

So it is with the gospel and the law. They are interspersed together, which brings about unity and holiness. They are inextricably entwined with one another. Luke tells us in his gospel chapter 16:16 (KJV) that the "law and prophets were until John: Since that time the kingdom of God is preached, and every man presses into it." In verse 17, directly following this, he said, "It is easier for heaven and earth to pass, than for one tittle of the law to fail." Matthew would concur in Matthew 5:17–18.

The law didn't just stop and grace take over—in the same sense as you would cut one thread and attach another in a weaving, although this technique is used quite often. Rather, it is where one thread is dropped as another is picked up, and the weaving continues in perfect harmony. The law was fulfilled by Christ, and grace has now become the dominant thread, by taking the forefront. As a result there is a beautiful interlay throughout this wonderful tapestry called justification and sanctification. In the same way there is also an exquisite stability and continuity between the law and grace. It isn't either/or. It is all seamlessly woven together as one. It is another one of those wonderful mysteries of the Bible that man may never be able to completely grasp this side of heaven.

224 Marguerite Porter Davison, *A Handweaver's Pattern Book*, revised ed. (Chadds Ford, PA: Margurite P. Davison, 1944).

The law and gospel intermingle in a beautiful dance in which each one totally augments the other as they move in unison to bring about the will of God. The law of the Old Testament and the gospel of the New Testament are not just linked but completely and thoroughly intertwined.[225] Each is saturated with God's grace. Even Campbell would go on to state, speaking of Galatians 5: "In Christ circumcision no longer matters. What does matter is faith expressing itself in love (Gal 5:17). While salvation is by faith in Christ and not by works, "genuine faith works itself out through love" (Eph 2:8–10, Jas 2:14–18).[226]

Possibly we could best describe this again by looking at a definition of the law itself. What do Christians mean when they speak of the law? Are they speaking of the old Mosaic laws? Those pertaining to the sacrificial, ceremonial, civil, judicial, and even dietary or the moral laws? If we look closely at the two commands Jesus gave His disciples, we see that they encompass the whole of the ten given at Sinai. John, speaking in First John, refers to these two commands of Jesus as the "law of love." As Christians we are to follow these two. Christians are more than willing to submit to these two commands of Jesus, or the "love" commands, while taking offense at any mention of the Ten Commandments. Does this make any sense apart from their image of the "ten," as representing something negative and restrictive to people? Jesus said in John 14:15, 20–21, 23 that if we keep His commands then we love Him.

If we pay attention to what is going on around us we may notice that lawlessness is increasing at an alarming rate, even within the walls of our churches. John says this is the spirit of antichrist. As humans we have always needed boundaries such as laws and rules. Hogan expresses it like this: "Like other logical laws, moral laws and

---

225 Lester L. Stephenson, *A Biblicist Law and View of the Law and Gospel* (Greenville, NC: Ambassador International) Kindle ed.

226 Donald K. Campbell, "Galatians" in *The Bible Knowledge Commentary: An Exposition of the Scriptures,* ed. J. F. Walvoord and R. B. Zuck (Wheaton, IL: Victor Books, 1985), Gal 5:4–6.

instincts are basic to well-functioning humans."[227] Imagine living in a country without laws.

In the book of Acts the leaders of the church in Jerusalem set some laws down for the new Gentiles who were entering the church on a daily basis as well as in great numbers. It might be mentioned that these were given in the early days of the church "grace" period. As Christians we still have boundaries, and we should view these as very positive. On the surface they may appear negative. But following them brings very positive results and a good life.

These rules handed down by the elders in Jerusalem may be considered as ceremonial matters, but they are more likely moral matters. The eating of the blood of animals refers back to Leviticus 18:6–20. The abstinence of sexual immorality refers to the marriage laws of Leviticus 18:6–10. Foods sacrificed to idols are referred to in 1 Corinthians 8–10 and Revelation 2:14, 20. Although these look back to the Jewish ceremonial law, Toussaint argues that they should be taken as "moral" laws, for the simple reason that it was a normal practice for Gentiles to use an idol temple for banquets and celebrations. Paul condemned these practices for Christian participation (1 Cor 10:14–22). Fornication was so common a sin among Gentiles that it was considered acceptable behavior. Christians also were involved in this type of activity as we can see by the New Testament injunctions against it (1 Cor 6:12–18). Paul evidently was answering some of these arguments that were in favor of immorality. The "third injunction about eating flesh without the blood being drained goes back further than Leviticus 17 to Genesis

---

[227] Paul Copan, "Does the Moral Argument Show There Is a God?" *The Apologetics Study Bible: Real Questions, Straight Answers, Stronger Faith*, ed. Ted Cabal, Chad Oven Brand (Nashville TN: Holman Bible Publishers, 2007), 1687.

9, where God established the Noahic Covenant, a 'contract' still in effect today."[228]

Toussaint contends that "all three of these prohibitions in Acts 15:20 are best taken in an ethical or moral sense. If this be so, they are still the responsibility of Christians today."[229]

Conclusion

In the church today there is a great deal of negative feelings about the law. Many state that it has no relationship to the Christian today. As well-rounded Christians we need to have a proper understanding of the law in the past as well as how it affects our lives today. Toussaint continues by pointing out that the relationship between the Old and New Testaments is necessary for our comprehension of God's word. "Many New Testament passages prove the validity of the Old Testament and the Law. Showing a true and genuine agreement between them." There are Old Testament passages that show foundational knowledge helping us to get a better picture of New Testament truth. And there are places in the New Testament that give us clarity on the Old Testament. We need both the law and the gospel together to get a complete picture of the scriptures.[230]

The law was never intended to be negative; in fact it is quite the opposite. God poured out His grace on the people of Israel through His law. No other nation or people on earth had laws or statutes like these. They didn't serve gods who cared about them like the God of Israel cared for His people (Dt 4:7–9). These laws were meant

---

[228] Stanley D. Toussaint, "Acts," in *The Bible Knowledge Commentary: An Exposition of the Scriptures,* ed. J. F. Walvoord and R. B. Zuck (Wheaton, IL: Victor Books, 1985), Acts 15:19–35, Logos Software.

[229] Ibid.

[230] Rick Ritchie, *What is This Law and Gospel Thing?* (*Modern Reformation,* March/April 1993), 7–11.

DR. SHIRLEY F. THURMAN

to bless the Israelites and to keep them safe. As a result of Israel's obedience, the whole world would be blessed (Gn 12).

For someone to say that the law was imperfect or was bad is to say that God Himself, who is perfect, could create something imperfect (which is impossible). It also chips away at the sovereignty of God (Dt 32:4).[231] The psalmist says of the law that it is good and right (Ps 19:1–11) and that the law is a delight for the soul.

It is this very same law that directs us even today in the way we should live. The Spirit Himself directs us toward the law. What the Old Testament tells us to do is to walk before God in His grace—to walk humbly, to do good, and to love mercy (Mi 6:8, Dt 10:12). Now that we are under grace, are we to ignore this? Remember, mercy after all is God's grace in action.

So as Christians we are to love the law of God and to seek to walk in holiness before our God. Williams would express that "while Christians are living under the covenant of grace, this does not release them from observing the fulfilled law as a rule of proper Christian living." He doesn't believe there is any opposition between the law and grace because the two are totally compatible. When Christ fulfilled the law He laid the foundation for grace, with the law still being in effect. It's just that now it is tempered by grace. The moral commands of the law, in its original form, are still applicable and binding today. Jesus fulfilled the law; He didn't abolish it. The Holy Spirit is the one operating by grace putting the law into the hearts of Christians, thereby enabling them to live in obedience.[232]

To think the law and the gospel are opposites is wrong thinking. Neither can we say that they are the same. Yet despite this, each is evident in the other while still being different. Despite this conundrum we understand that "both Testaments contain the revelation of one God, given to people through faith and who are

---

[231] Lester L. Stephenson.
[232] A. Lukyn Williams, *Matthew*, vol.1 in the *Pulpit Commentary,* ed. Spence and Joseph Exell (New York: Funk & Wagnalls, 1913), 157.

sustained by his grace. They are His covenant people and they persevere in faith."[233]

Needless to say there is so much more to be discovered, but this is not meant to be an exhaustive study of the subject. Just suffice it to say that keeping the law does not justify the believer, for that is by faith in Christ. But it does have much to do with the way one conducts himself or herself as a Christian.

So next we are going to take a closer look at antinomianism.

---

[233] John Murray, *Principles of Conduct* (Grand Rapids, MI: Eerdmans, 1957), in *Five Views of Law and the Gospel*, Stanley N. Gundry, ed. (Grand Rapids, MI: Zondervan, 1996), 16.

8
CHAPTER

Antinomianism

Now we are going to take a little different peek at the law and the gospel by looking at the two main antagonists—namely antinomianism and legalism. Both of these are deadly to the Christian message. We often think of them as two extremes in opposition to one another, or as opposite poles. But are they? Sproul makes the point that these are "twin distortions of authentic righteousness which have plagued the church from the beginning. The New Testament documents reveal that struggles with both Legalism and Antinomianism were both common in the New Testament church."[234]

From this we can see that rather than being in direct opposition to one another as it appears at face value, the reality is somewhat different. They are quite similar. One could go so far as to say they are two sides of the same coin. Where legalism says that we must keep the law for our justification, antinomianism states that once we are free in Christ we no longer have need of the law. They cannot both be right. Might one be right and the other wrong, or could

---

[234] R.C. Sproul, *Following Christ* (Wheaton, IL: Tyndale House, 1996).

they both be wrong? As such it then becomes our responsibility to ferret out the truth.

While the scribes and Pharisees at the time of Jesus appeared to be such devoted doers of the law, it appears that they were nothing of the sort. Jesus confronted them with their hypocrisy in Matthew 23:23, concerning their habit of tithing even their mint, anise, and cummin to the smallest detail while neglecting the weightier matters of the law such as judgment, mercy, and faith. This demonstrates that they too were lawbreakers or antinomian in their actions. Through their selective obedience they were actually being disobedient, and their legalism resulted in antinomian behavior.[235] One could say that they are different while they are the same.

We might be inclined to try to find a middle ground between these two extremes. After all haven't we all heard that somewhere between license and legalism is liberty? But what if we find there really is no middle ground?

We need to find a better solution. Mark Jones states that there can be no middle ground between them because they are fundamentally the same error, just dressed up differently. These two, as stated earlier by Sproul, are "twin heresies."[236] O'Donovan implies they are theological, both in nature and of Christological importance.[237] As such they both undermine the teaching of the gospel. Neither of these views could be further from the truth set forth in the Bible.

We hear much in our churches today about the evils of legalism, creating familiarity with the term. Most Christians have a pretty clear understanding of what it is. But just as serious if not more so is the teaching of antinomianism. What exactly is antinomianism? The word itself, *anti*, means against the law. It is a compound word taken from the two words. The word from Latin is *antinomus*, which

---

[235] Mark Jones, *Antinomianism: Reformed Theology's Unwelcome Guest* (Phillipsburg, NJ: P&R Publishing, 2013), 2–3.

[236] Sproul, *Following Christ*.

[237] Oliver O'Donovan, *Ressurection and Moral Order: An Outline for Evangelical Ethics* (Leicester Apollos, 1996), 12.

means anti. We might understand it better as "against or opposed to." The other is from the Greek word *nomos*, meaning law. In short, antilaw, or opposed to the law, or one who breaks the law, a lawbreaker.[238] According to Manser it is a form of spiritual anarchy that rejects the law as having any place in the Christian walk either as an instructor or as an assessor.[239] Antinomianism then is an outright rejection of God's laws (Jer 2:20, Hos 8:12, 2 Pt 2:10).

Steele explains: "The root of this error of Antinomianism is a false view of the Mediatorial work of Christ." Namely that Jesus Himself performed the obedience that is required of the believer. As a result God cannot justly demand anything further from redeemed men. Christ's righteousness is imputed to the believer in such a way as to excuse him of any and all sin that may be committed by the believer after justification. The assumption being that the believer is no longer accountable for his sin after conversion. Modern Universalism is yet another form of antinomianism. This is understood as justification through Christ without obedience to the law or the gospel.[240]

Karleen believes that antinomianism then would be any position based on a mistaken view that rejects God's law as binding on the Christian today.[241]

This error, as McDonald points out, is a distorted view of grace. It is a view that makes chaos of order and deceives many Christians by assuring them of salvation while living in lawlessness. This

[238] Merriam-Webster, *Merriam-Webster's Collegiate Dictionary,* 11th ed. (Springfield, MA: Merriam-Webster, 2003).

[239] Martin H. Manser, *Dictionary of Bible Themes: The Accessible and Comprehensive Tool for Topical Studies* (London: Martin Manser, 2009), Logos Software.

[240] Daniel Steele STD, *For Holiness or Antinomianism, Revised: The Theology of the So-Called Plymouth Brethren Examined and Refuted* (Christian Witness Publishing, 1899), Kindle location 285.

[241] Paul S. Karleen, *The Handbook to Bible Study: With a Guide to the Scofield Study System* (New York: Oxford University Press, 1987), 310.

undermines the church and God's word.[242] It is anathema to the body of Christ. It is destructive, deceiving, and detestable. This is not the same grace that is taught in scripture.

Christians have been set free from the shackles of sin and death with the death and resurrection of Jesus (Jn 8:34, Rom 6:14–23). They have been supernaturally regenerated by the power of the Holy Spirit at their conversion (Rom 6:18, 22). In Christ, believers are no longer slaves to the sin that formerly governed their lives. As a result they are now free in Christ to do His good will. The Holy Spirit Himself will give them the power to live for Him (Mt 7:12). Paul says we "serve in the new way of the Spirit, and not in the old way of a written code" (Rom 7:6 NIV). Sin no longer has dominion over those who put their trust in Christ to save them. J. I. Packer says that the sin that once ruled their lives through acts of disobedience and a constant lack of passion for law-keeping, has now been replaced with a new heart. This heart is motivated by gratitude and grace fully empowered by the Holy Spirit (Jer 31:33, Ez 36:26–27).[243]

As seen earlier in chapter 6, man cannot even begin to comprehend the extent of God's grace or the compassion with which it was delivered. Yet, it is safe to say that this marvelous grace came at a horrendous price. Therefore, it is not to be cheapened by a life lived in the flesh after conversion. When Paul was asked in Romans 6:1 (NIV), if they could demonstrate God's grace more fully by continuing in their sin, his instant reply was, "God Forbid!" Quite the contrary, in verse 2 he goes on to explain how they had died to sin; therefore, how could they live any longer in it?

It is the life lived in victory, no longer controlled by sin and the flesh that brings glory to God. As opposed to one lived in darkness,

---

242 W. McDonald, *Introduction to, For Holiness or Antinomianism, Revised: The Theology of the So-Called Plymouth Brethren Examined and Refuted*, by Daniel Steele, STD (Christian Witness Publishers, 1899), Kindle location, 274.

243 J. I. Packer, *Concise Theology: A Guide to Historic Christian Beliefs* (Wheaton, IL: Tyndale House, 1993), Logos.

dishonor, shame, and defeat. His grace is so large and so good that it extends far beyond the first step of washing away our sin at Calvary, although that is a glorious starting place. We just need to know and understand that sin, which was defeated there, is washed away and gone. God has graciously given believers a do over. Not so we can continue in our former lifestyle of sin and lawlessness that brought us to the cross in the first place. Rather He supplies us with the grace to be able to start over with a new life of service and surrender to God.

This grace that washes our sins away extends forward then from Calvary into our daily lives, pouring out grace upon grace to help Christians live a life free of that sin. This grace is so much more than just covering of our sin. The sacrifices in the Old Testament covered our sins, never freeing us, just covering over them until the next sacrifice could be made. Jesus's death and resurrection did something much greater (Heb 10:1–14). Anderson thinks it eradicated the fear of death for those who believe on the name of Jesus to save them. Sin would no longer tower above a Christian when he or she believed on Christ. That same grace of God is being extended to us through the Holy Spirit residing within us. It is that power that grants to us the ability to live a life that is pleasing to Him and brings Him glory and honor (Rom 8:7–8).[244]

As we can see, antinomianism has been around for a long time. Just about as soon as Luther came to the revelation or rediscovery of our salvation being by faith alone, one of his followers, John Agricola (1492–1566), turned it into a license for sin.[245] According to Johann Schneider, "Agricola emphasized Luther's principle that Christians are under the gospel rather than under the law. As early as 1527 he was already in controversy with Philip Melanchton (Luther's colleague), concerning the place of the Ten Commandments in

---

244 Richard Anderson, *No Holiness, No Heaven* (Carlyle, PA: Banner of Truth Trust, 1986), 41.

245 Daniel Steele, STD, *For Holiness or Antinomianism Revived*, 344.

Christian experience, where it was said that Agricola found no place for them."[246]

Luther himself would be the one to coin the term *antinomianism* because of a denial of any role for the law in Christian living.[247] It should be noted by Steele that Luther was not an antinomian.[248] Lloyd James said of Luther in reference to Antinomianism that "in his day he would call this a blasphemous heresy."[249]

Theologians of the sixteenth and seventeenth centuries had much to say about this topic. Charles Hodges would tell us that during the Reformation, antinomianism never had much hold in the churches, simply because they didn't see any great disconnect from their moral duties and any system that would teach that "Christ is a Savior as well from the power as from the penalty of sin." In order to be a partaker of the benefit of His death, one also needs to be a partaker of the power of His life, holding to the divine authority of scripture, which declares that "without holiness no man shall see the Lord" (Heb 12:14).[250] In 1 Corinthians 6:9–10, Paul, that great champion of faith, says, "Be not deceived; neither fornicators, nor idolater, nor adulterers, nor effeminate, nor abusers of themselves with mankind, nor thieves, nor covetous, nor drunkards, nor revilers, nor extortioners shall inherit the kingdom of God."

Who was Paul speaking to? He was speaking to the Christians in Corinth, many of whom he says had been previously doers of these things before coming to Christ (1 Cor 6). These things had been repented of and should have been left behind in their new walk

---

[246] Johann Schneider, *Agricola in Who's Who in Christian History,* ed. J. D. Douglass and Philip W. Comfort (Wheaton, IL: Tyndale House, 1992), 7–8.

[247] Schneider, 7–8.

[248] Steele, Kindle location, 348.

[249] D. M. Lloyd-Jones, *Darkness and Light: An Exposition of Ephesians 4:17–5:17* (Pennsylvania: Banner of Truth, 1982), 348.

[250] Charles Hodge, *Systematic Theology,* vol. 3 (Oak Harbor, WA: Logos Research Systems, 1997), 241.

with Christ. What does this tell us about how we should live after becoming Christians? If this was true for the church in Corinth, is it no longer true today?

Once again this heresy of heresies is arising in our churches under the guise of "grace." A supposedly "new wave" on the Christian scene is known as "hyper-grace, radical grace, greasy grace or the new reformation of grace. In many cases it is taking the church by storm. It is insidious and maybe the most dangerous teaching in the church in this present day. Mike Bickle says we are "living in a crucial hour when deception is sweeping into the church through a distorted message of grace."[251] This "teaching" is really antinomianism in disguise, just dressed up to look appealing. After all, what Christian in his or her right mind could properly protest "grace?"

The premise of this "new grace" is to reject any form of the law simply because we are now in Christ and therefore perfect in God's eyes. No sin past, present, or future can touch us because we once said yes to God, and therefore all is already forgiven. Nor is repentance required for salvation, as in many cases this is seen as a "work." We can live in any manner we choose, because God is so in love with us that He no longer sees our sin.[252]

Dr. Robert Anderson, a new "Gracer," in his book states that there is no place in the gospel for the preaching or teaching of repentance for salvation.[253] This also is an undermining of the gospel message. Therefore, we should be asking ourselves, really? Jesus taught the necessity of repentance when He warned the unbelieving Jews: "unless you repent, you too will all perish" (Lk 13:3). He had His disciples preaching repentance among all the nations.[254]

---

[251]   Mike Bickle, founder of IHOP-KC. *Introduction to Hypergrace by Dr. Michael Brown*, Kindle edition.

[252]   Dr. Michael Brown, *Hyper-Grace: Exposing the Dangers of the Modern Grace Message*, Kindle edition.

[253]   Robert Anderson. *The Gospel and Its Ministry* (1907), 58.

[254]   No Holiness, No Heaven, 48.

Again we need to understand that repentance is necessary for salvation. Repentance is a turning away or doing a U-turn in our lives. According to Oden, "Repentance remains a vital Christian doctrine."[255] The narrow way mentioned in the Bible begins with repentance (2 Cor 7:10). "Repentance by its nature requires a change of heart as well as direction.[256] Justification is incomplete or insincere if it does not lead to a new life."[257] The biblical view of repentance is not something man can produce. The ability to do so once again comes from God's grace and the work of the Holy Spirit. It is a gift of God to all who believe (Acts 5:31, 11:18). God gets all the credit not us. Oden continues with: "This Faith comes from God. It enables freedom of action and trust. This righteousness comes from God thru faith in Jesus Christ to all who believe."[258] "Our part is to accept this great gift by acknowledging our sinful state and our need of a savior, by confession, and repenting of our sin and placing our faith in Christ to save us."[259] Jesus still calls us to repentance today just as Peter called those present on the day of Pentecost to repent (Acts 2:38). Repentance is still a crucial doctrine in the church today. This repentance is not just a changing of one's mind as hypergrace teaches. Rather it is a change of direction in one's mind, heart, and ultimately actions.

The teaching of antinomianism seems to be confusing the doctrine of salvation or justification with sanctification, which is another work of God's grace to the believer just as justification is. Justification is by faith alone, just as Luther taught—where sanctification is the task where the believer has a part. This is where God enables our obedient response through His grace as we continue

---

[255] Oden, 567.

[256] Ibid.

[257] Ibid.

[258] Oden, 607.

[259] Oden, 659.

to walk in that grace. Again, Oden said, "God does not believe for us, but simply enables us to believe."[260]

Obviously antinomianism is not the same grace as that taught in the Bible. Regardless of what it is called or how it is displayed, Manser claims it is still that same lawless form of anarchy. [261] So although we may not hear the term from the pulpit (antinomianism), we can know that it is still very much alive and well today.

What is it about antinomianism that makes it so dangerous, besides it being seductive and alluring to the flesh? It conveys the message that once a person becomes a Christian then there are no changes expected in one's behavior—that Christians are free to continue in their sins. Scripture does not tell us this. On the contrary if a person is born again there are changes. Some of those changes are immediate while others require work or discipline in the life of the believer (Phil 2:12). Jesus's blood saves us from the bondage of sin; we are free from its grasp; we are delivered from the oppression of death and sin (1 Jn: 5, Rom 8:1–10). We certainly are not made perfect in God's sight if we continue in the same old habitual sin that He died to set us free from as antinomianism suggests. This is a gross error.

In the book of Jude we are told in verse 3: "Beloved, when I gave all diligence to write to you of the common salvation, it was good for me to write to you, and exhort you that ye should earnestly contend for the faith which was once delivered unto the saints." This is an interesting choice of words encouraging and warning them to earnestly contend for the faith. Why do we suppose this was necessary? Well, verse 4 explains why. "For there are certain men crept in unawares, who were before of old ordained to this condemnation, ungodly men, turning the grace of our God into lasciviousness, and denying the only Lord God and our Lord Jesus Christ."

[260] Oden, 607
[261] Manser, *Dictionary of Bible Theme*, Logos.

Antinomians? In the first century? These men were trying to misuse God's grace for their own agenda. Jude mentions the faith once and for all delivered. This is such an interesting phrase. According to Dr. Michael Brown this new "Radical-grace," we are hearing so much about today in our churches teaches that this is all about a new revelation or understanding of grace completely overlooked by the saints of old.[262] Notice, there is a note of finality in Jude's words "once and for all." Manser answers that "there is no longer a need for new revelation as it was once and for all delivered to the saints."[263]

Dunnet comments: Doctrine should not be held as a detachment from life. God Himself has given the church the responsibility to keep the Gospel intact, as a sacred trust (Gal 1:6–9; 1 Tm 1:19, 6:3, 20–21; 2 Tm 11:13–14). If one's doctrine is correct it will correspond in holy living, so as not to lose the practical purpose. This appears to be the error confronting Jude—antinomianism or "lawless libertinism, that leads to a denial of the place of the law in the life of the Christian."[264]

This is not to say that there isn't some truth in the antinomian view. On the contrary that is what makes this so perilous. But a half-truth can be just as dangerous as an outright lie and in many cases more so because the truth is twisted in such a fashion as to say something completely different from which it was intended. Let's take a little closer look, and see what it really is. This is a deception. After the Reformation it was given a name and considered heresy of the highest order. So why are we so quick to accept it without question today? Here are some things we should keep in mind about this doctrine.

---

[262] Dr. Michael Brown, *Hyper-Grace*, Kindle location 269–74.

[263] Manser, *Dictionary of Bible Themes.*

[264] Walter M. Dunnett, *Exploring the New Testament* (Wheaton, IL: Crossway Books, 2001), 91.

Manson is quick to point out these four things to keep in mind.

- Grace will never lead us to sin (Rom 6:1–2, 15; Rom 3:5–6; Gal 2:17–21).
- We must resist sin (Rom 6:12, 14; Heb 12:1–2; 1 Jn 5:16–18).
- The law remains valid for believers today (Mt 5:17–18, Prv 28:7, Rom 7:12, 1 Tm 1:8).
- The danger of falling back into sin (Rom 6:1–2, Heb 12:1, 1 Jn 1:8–10.)[265]

Basically antinomianism says that Christians are no longer under any laws—moral or otherwise. They teach that once saved it matters not how the Christian acts, as God no longer sees his sin. This is not even an issue of eternal security in Christ so much as it is one of lawlessness in the life of a believer. Where one can continue in his or her sin with complete impunity because of an erroneous view of Jesus's righteousness imputed to the sinner covering all sin past, present, and future. It might be noted that this is very interesting in light of the fact that Jesus never sinned. Nor would He or His Holy Spirit ever lead a Christian into sin.

Jesus Himself was obedient even to the death on the cross, yet scripture says without sin. One might think that would be incentive enough to cause one to want to live an obedient life. Such is not the case, which we will cover shortly. When we come to the realization that we have been freed by Christ not to do as we please but to be conformed to the image of Christ, it changes everything (Rom 12:1–2). Drane explains that this transformation that takes place is the distinct work of the Holy Spirit in our lives empowering us not only to live for Christ but giving us the desire to want to do so.[266]

---

[265] Manser, *Dictionary of Bible Themes*.
[266] John William Drane, *Introducing the New Testament*, completely revised and updated (Oxford: Lion Publishing, 2000), 339–40.

Something else antinomianism teaches is that at conversion all our sins are forgiven—past, present, and future.[267] Christ certainly died to forgive our sins—those of which we were guilty. The only way it can be said He paid for our sins of the present and future is if we confess and ask Him for forgiveness. In that sense it can be said He has made provision for our sins of the present and future. However, it is how that provision is appropriated that is in question. If we confess our sins (acknowledge them and turn from them) He has promised that He will forgive all our sins.

The question might be raised as to how exactly can one be forgiven for sins not yet committed? Unconfessed sin? The Bible does not teach this. We cannot say that we have no sin, because scripture says to say that is to be a liar (1 Jn 1:8). We still have a sinful nature that we have to bring under submission to Christ (2 Cor 10:5–6). It is interesting that in 1 John chapter 1 it says that God wishes that none of us would sin. So we know it is His will that we do not sin. It goes on to say that if we do, then we have an advocate with the father, and if we will confess those sins He is faithful and just and will forgive them and cleanse us from all unrighteousness. Again, how does God forgive unconfessed sin? It is only as we confess sins that God forgives them.

This assures us that God will indeed forgive future sins we may commit, but it is not assured without confession of those sins. To confess basically means to agree with God. God is holy, and He hates sin, and it is unacceptable in His sight. Therefore we must confess our sins so that then He will forgive. First John 1:6 says very plainly "that if we claim to have fellowship with him and yet walk in darkness, we lie and do not live out the truth." Verse 7 tells us: "But, if we walk in the light, as he is in the light, we have fellowship with one another, and the blood of Jesus, his Son purifies us from all sin." If, in verse 8, we claim as Antinomianism does to no longer have any sin or to be above sin, then we are liars and deceived, and the word

---

[267] Steele, Kindle location 242.

is not in us. From there he moves into verse 9, which tells us that if we confess our sin He is faithful and just to forgive those sins and then cleanse us from all unrighteousness. We should take note that in verses 6, 7, and 9 we find the word "*if.*" It is an interesting word because it means something is conditional. If we do something, then some particular action will follow. It is not a given; it is conditional on our actions.

This is a far cry from the belief that every sin a Christian may commit from the day of conversion is totally ignored, regardless of how egregious the sin may be. This doctrine is precariously deceptive to have ingrained in the minds of Christians. The idea that they do not have to ever be concerned about committing sin again because God has already forgiven it is fallacious, ludicrous, and unscriptural.[268] God is not going to bless our sin before or after conversion. Nor will He turn a blind eye to sin, just because we "believe," in Him. He saved us for something better—namely to live a holy life. He didn't save us to patch up our old sinful life, just so we could continue our lives as they were before coming to Him.

It is true that all faithful believers will at some point in their lives stumble and fall. It is with the assurance that when we acknowledge that sin for what it is and ask for forgiveness and turn from it, God will hear and forgive us and clean us up (1 Jn 1:9). Not for the purpose of continuing along those lines, but to help us to free ourselves of it. It's called repentance, and, yes, despite what antinomianism and the radical grace preachers are teaching in our churches today, the saints are also called to repent (2 Tm 2:25, Heb 6:6, 2 Pt 3:9). Jesus when asked by the disciples to teach them to pray, taught them to ask forgiveness for their trespasses just as they were supposed to forgive others (Mt 6:9–13). He even told them that if they were preparing to take communion and realized that someone had something against them, they should hurry and make things right with them so that they themselves could be forgiven (Mt 5:24) and so that things

---

[268] Brown, "Hyper-grace," Kindle location, 855.

would go well with them. It might be pointed out that if they did not forgive others, God wouldn't forgive them either.

It would be unfair to say that all Antinomians live ungodly lives. Many of them do live godly lives, having recognized that in being saved they have been delivered from their old lives. Nor are all Antinomians living in open rebellion with regard to the law. It is just that they see no connection with the law. There is no sense of its relativity or value for the Christian under the new covenant. It is as though it does not exist, vanished, abolished, dead and gone, never to return. Just a total disconnect with the law.

Now not to be misconstrued let it be said that there is no suggestion here that if you hold Antinomian views then you are not a Christian. It is the doctrine of Antinomianism that is so hazardous to the believer, encouraging others to live in their sin while offering them a false hope of salvation.

Scripture teaches that the law is holy, right, and perfect (Rom 7:11–13, Ps 19) even for the believer nowadays. God's laws, precepts, and decrees have not changed or become obsolete. The law just holds a different place in the life of a believer today. It still convicts us and points us to Christ. The law never saved us, nor will it, but it is a good guide and gives us good solid instruction in how we should live our lives in Christ if we could just visualize the law as God's loving protection. If we follow it, there is blessing and protection, and warnings to keep us safe and on the right path. It is like a guardrail on a high mountain pass that keeps us from falling off the edge of the cliffs on high treacherous roads. If we choose to ignore that guardrail, we do so at our own peril. It is there to protect us and warn us of danger for a purpose. The law gives us guidance and wisdom as we travel life's road. God has set boundaries on everything in His creation—the heavens and planets, the earth, and the sea (Jb: chapter 38). Would He be so lax as to not give His finest creations boundaries, for their safety and well-being? When Christians seek to observe God's moral laws in their lives it should not be mistaken for salvation by works, nor is it legalism. It is instead grace at work within us.

At the moment we are justified, we begin our journey into the realm of sanctification, and as such we are to begin walking in that marvelous grace, no longer in bondage. Calvin said, "We are justified by faith alone—but the faith that justifies is never alone."[269] Anderson concurs with: "True saving faith is always accompanied by a holy life and by good works. Justification of necessity entails sanctification."[270] Robert McCheyne puts it this way: "If Christ justifies you, He will sanctify you. He will not save you and leave you in your sins."[271]

Conclusion

Antinomianism would teach us that we go from justification straight to glorification without any need of sanctification. Scripture does not bear this out. In fact this doctrine greatly undermines the Word. While we all agree that the law is no longer the means to our salvation that does not mean the law isn't a powerful witness and guide for our sanctification. It is the means for us to see and recognize our sin so that we may be convicted and repent. It is a wise and useful tool for the Christian in that it leads us into ways that are pleasing to God. Yes, there are ways in which the Christian can please God and just as many ways to displease and anger Him.

The deception and danger is that there are probably many folks who call themselves Christians simply because they said the sinner's prayer many years back or walked down the aisle at a church service and prayed with someone and then believed themselves to be saved when it is possible they were never justified in the first place. It is safe to say that if we are not being sanctified on a daily basis, then we were probably never justified to begin with. This type of teaching encourages slothful behavior by stressing that there is no need for

---

269   John Calvin, quoted from *No Holiness, No Heaven*, 3.

270   Anderson, *No Holiness, No Heaven*, 3.

271   Robert Murray McCheyne, quote from *No Holiness, No Heaven*, 3.

a believer to strive to live a better life but rather to continue on in their sin thinking God is greatly pleased with their behavior. Again we must ask ourselves what scripture says. In Romans 8:7–8 Paul tells us that "the sinful mind is hostility to God. It does not submit to God's law, nor can it do so. Those controlled by the sinful nature cannot please God." Anderson speaking on this verse says, "This is man the rebel against God's rule, man the lawbreaker, man the Antinomian."[272] Again, in Ephesians 5:6, Paul tells them: "Let no one deceive you with empty words. For because of such things God's wrath comes on those who are disobedient." In Galatians 6:7, Paul again warns the Galatians: "Be not deceived for God is not mocked, for whatsoever a man sows that also shall he reap."

So as Christians washed by the blood of Jesus at Calvary and having had our sins forgiven, let us encourage one another in the faith. We are saved by faith, and we are called to a "walk." Paul encourages us to walk worthy of the vocation in which we were called (Eph 4:1, Col 1:10–11, 1 Thes 2:12). Now why would he say that? This is so that we might live our lives pleasing God by our behavior (Col 1:10). We know that the lives we lead speak much louder than our words do. Let our words ring true and our testimony be established by the lives we live before God and man, through God's grace and the empowerment of the Holy Spirit.

This is what brings glory and honor to God. Yes, we slip and fall. Yet, again the good news is that when we do, we have Jesus as our advocate with the Father, and if we will just confess He will forgive us and reestablish us in His righteousness (1 Jn 1:8–9). What a glorious promise—that He will indeed forgive those future sins when they reveal themselves in our lives if we will just confess them.

God's grace is so magnificent that through His Holy Spirit He has given us all we need to live for Him. May God give us more of His grace and the desire to honor Him in all we say and do.

---

[272] Anderson, *No Holiness, No Heaven*, 41.

R. C. Sproul explains that we can practice ungodly practices and flee to God's sovereignty for safety, laying the blame on God and His unchanging will. Sproul says this "is the spirit of Antichrist, that spirit of lawlessness, or antinomianism, that despises God's law and ignores his precepts." He also points out that Protestants are particularly vulnerable to this distortion when "we seek refuge in our precious doctrine of justification by faith alone, forgetting that the very doctrine is to be a catalyst for the pursuit of righteousness and obedience to the perceptive will of God."[273]

Justification and sanctification are two separate works of God's grace in the believer's life. Antinomians tend to forget this, wrapping the two up as one when in reality they are separate. Justification is a legal term where all those charges against us are dropped and forever purged from the record. This happens right when we repent. Sanctification happens at the same time but is different in the sense that it is not just a onetime happening so much as it is progressive in its nature (Phil 2:12). The Holy Spirit begins a new work in us upon our conversion, to transform and sanctify us through His word (Jn 17, Rom 12:1–2).

The next issue we are going to tackle is legalism, the other side of the coin. This is equally destructive to the believer and the church.

---

[273] R. C. Sproul, *Following Christ.*

9
CHAPTER

Legalism

Having worked our way through antinomianism, one would be inclined to think that legalism would be a cinch. But alas, this is not the case. In many ways legalism for the Christian can be even craftier and more dangerous. Whereas one for the most part can spot the errors prevalent in antinomianism, this is a little more difficult where legalism is concerned.

If anything, it would be much easier for Christians to fall into legalism simply because of their desire to do what is right and pleasing to the Lord.

Before we roll up our sleeves and enter into a full assault on legalism, let's step back and take a good long look at what legalism is not. There seems to be some confusion among Christians as to what constitutes legalism. It is very popular today that whenever Christians are confronted with something they do not like to hear or something that convicts them, they immediately pull the legalism card. In our politically correct culture this has become all too common. So by looking at what isn't legalism we may be better equipped to catch a glimpse of legalism for the deadly thing it is.

What legalism is *not*:

- Telling someone that he or she is a sinner and in need of a savior is *not* legalism.
- Telling someone that if he or she continues on his or her present course that destruction lies ahead is *not* legalism.
- Calling someone to give an account of his or her actions is *not* legalism.
- Counseling two young people in love that moving in together is not the best choice for them is *not* legalism.
- A Christian who is trying to live a holy life or one who may be trying to observe God's moral laws merely because he or she loves God and His word is *not* legalism.
- Telling someone that it is wrong to be involved in an adulterous affair is *not* legalism.
- Explaining to someone that gossiping, lying, stealing, or bearing false witness is sin is *not* legalism.
- Telling the truth about Jesus and the scripture and asking people to repent is *not* legalism.
- Loving God's law is *not* legalism.
- Confronting someone spreading heresy is *not* legalism.

Knowles would have us to know that where legalism binds us in fearful and obsessive effort, the love for God's law sets us free. It shields us from the opinions of others and safeguards us from self-deceit. It guides us away from wrongdoing, hurtful consequences, and guilt. It releases us to do what is right and pleasing in the Lord's sight.[274]

As Christians we need to speak the truth of the word of God in season and out, when it is popular to do so and when it is not. Yes, by all means we need to do it in love, as this does not give us license to be unkind or cruel.

---

[274] Andrew Knowles, *The Bible Guide,* 1st Ausburg Books ed. (Minneapolis, MN: Augsburg, 2001), 245.

Yet we need to understand that the truth is important. The truth of scripture has not changed nor will it. It is this truth that sets us free, and although the truth can and does hurt sometimes, it is the medicine that heals. John said the law was up until Christ, and in Him came truth and grace (Jn 1:17). How wonderful that the truth came, but it didn't come alone; it came with grace. Isn't that a wonderful thought? The truth that can seem so harsh was saddled with grace so that it might not overwhelm us.

The difference is that to add anything else to the grace of God in order to obtain salvation is legalism, such as being baptized in order to be saved. The thief on the cross is an interesting story because he had no chance for baptism, yet Jesus assured him that he would be with Him in heaven that very day. Baptism is an important act of obedience but simply as a witness to the world and other believers of the work that has already taken place inside. It is a believer's baptism, not something we do to be saved, as baptism does not save us. To do this would be legalism just as telling someone they must worship on Saturday instead of Sunday to be saved. Some would have us believe that they should read the King James Bible only, or they are doomed, etc. Legalism is basically Jesus plus anything else deemed necessary for salvation. Trying to keep God's law in order to be justified is putting the cart before the horse and is legalism. It is after we are saved and God's Spirit resides within us that we have a desire to follow His commands. We don't do it in order to be saved as that is impossible apart from Christ.

Wiersbe poses the question that seems to perplex the Christian today: "Does this mean that the Old Testament law has no ministry to New Testament Christians?" Of course not. The law still reveals the holiness of God, and in the law Jesus Christ can be seen (Lk 24:27). "We know that the Law is good if a man uses it properly" (1 Tm 1:8, NIV). The Law reveals sin and warns of the consequences of sin, but it has no power to prevent sin or redeem the sinner. Only grace can do that."[275] So we can see that the law still has a place in the life of a Christian, but it needs to be in its proper place as teacher, revealer of sin, and guide. It has been superseded at the cross. As a result it no longer has the dominate role in the life of a believer as it did in the Old Testament. Now that Christ has paid the atonement for sin, the law has taken a back seat, as it were. It wasn't thrown out of the vehicle, as we still need it to lead us into paths of righteousness and to keep us from falling, but we no longer need to keep it for the purposes of justification.

What we need to do is take a closer look at exactly what legalism was in Jesus's day and what we see it as today. Is there a difference, and if so, what might it be?

According to E. P. Saunders: "Ever since the reformation, scholars have understood New Testament writers, and Paul in particular, to be opposing Jewish legalism, which taught that one could merit right standing before God by doing the works of the law. His contention was that "scholarship has read Paul and Second Temple Judaism through the lenses of the Reformation struggle between Protestantism and Roman Catholicism instead of from a historical perspective." Saunders further claims that "there is no evidence of legalism that can be supported from the Jewish texts themselves, with the exception of Ezra 4. As a result the idea that Judaism was legalistic is a serious misreading of the evidence."[276]

Saunders goes on to state the Jews were not following the law by faith; they were following them by their trusting in their works (Rom 9:32). They were not yielding to God to save them by His power. They wanted to save themselves by their own righteousness (Rom 10:3)."[277]

---

[275] Warren W. Wiersbe, *The Bible Exposition Commentary* (Wheaton, IL: Victor Books, 1996), Col 2:17.

[276] E. P. Saunders, *Paul and Palestinian Judaism: A Comparison of Patterns of Religion* (Minneapolis, MN: Fortress Press, 2017), Kindle ed.

[277] Ibid.

God's law was always meant to be laws of love—love for God and love for other people. Somewhere along the way it was altered by men who would rather work for their salvation than put their faith in God. J. I. Packer would express it this way: legalism by definition is a "distortion of obedience."[278] As Christians we all know it is much easier to follow a set of rules than it is to love our neighbors. It is clear to see how this thinking could easily infect the body today, especially as we see the world becoming more and more vile. There was, however, much more involved here. For the legalist who is following the law or the rules and regulations of a group or leader, it becomes more important than the truth of God's word. This then becomes an idol. God did not call us to more rules and regulations. He has called us to faith in Christ and into a relationship with Him through His son, followed by a special relationship with other believers in Him.

Eugene H. Merrill put it this way:

> The oneness and exclusivity of Yahweh demand that He be loved by His people with a love that is synonymous with covenant fidelity. But love for God cannot be divorced from love for others, especially for the disadvantaged. Thus the center and substance of the covenant relationship is not legalism but love.[279]

This clearly teaches us that even the Mosaic Covenant was about love. The laws God gave on Sinai were laws of love. Somewhere along the line they just got twisted into something more sinister. First, when we love God with our whole heart and soul and mind

---

[278] J. I. Packer, *Concise Theology: A Guide to Historic Christian Beliefs* (Wheaton, IL: Tyndale House, 1993), 175–77.

[279] Eugene H. Merrill, "The Pentateuch" in *Holman Concise Bible Commentary,* ed. David S. Dockery (Nashville, TN: Broadman & Holman, 1998), 65–66.

He changes our perspective in every aspect of our lives. Second, if we love others we will always look out for their best interest as we do our own. These were the principles of the Old Testament law just as they are of the New Testament.

Only now due to our freedom from the overriding burden of sin in our lives we are set free to put these laws into action. This is not something we can do; God has done it for us. The Jews took these simple laws of love and turned them into something quite different—something binding, and it enslaved them. Only Christ can set us free from these things. We need to be careful in Christ that we do not do the same thing with ourselves and others.

Shreiner's view says that Paul didn't believe that the law could be fulfilled in one's own strength, either, believing that fulfilling the law was due to the inward work of the Holy Spirit, which enabled believers to obey God's commandments (Rom 2:25–29, 8:4, 13:8–10; Gal 5:2–6, 14; 1 Cor 7:19).[280] If it was impossible for the Jews to save themselves by trying to keep the law, why would Christians today believe that it is possible? This defies good common sense. There is only one remedy for legalism, and that is Christ. Paul said he preached only Jesus and Him crucified. We need to do the same and nothing more. Do we make things too complicated today?

According to Wiersbe, it is through God's grace that we are saved, and when a person lives by grace, he or she depends on the power of the Holy Spirit whereas with the law they must depend on their own work.[281] We cannot do it, or we would have done it centuries ago, and then the sacrifice of Jesus wouldn't have been needed. Nonetheless, it couldn't be done, and Jesus stepped down from heaven and made our salvation possible. All we need to do is confess our sin, believe in Him, and place our trust in Him to save us.

---

[280] T. R. Schreiner, "In the New Testament," in *New Bible Dictionary,* ed. D. R. W. Wood, I. H. Marshall, A. R. Millard, et al., 3rd ed. (Leicester, England, Downers Grove, IL: Inter Varsity Press, 1996), 676–77.

[281] Wiersbe.

John MacArthur claims while speaking of the time of Jesus that the nation of Israel for all intents and purposes had become apostate. Judaism of that day was corrupt. It was no longer the faith of Abraham but was totally legalistic and hypocritical, full of self-righteous works and rules.[282]

Drane informs us that the law was never the actual basis of the Old Testament faith, nor for that matter is it entirely absent from the New Testament. They both place the law in the context of a covenant understanding where God's love is the foundation principle.[283]

Webster's defines legalism as a noun:

1. Strict, literal, or excessive conformity to the law or to a religious or moral code (the institutionalized legalism that restricts free choice).
2. A legal term or rule.

A legalist is:

1. An advocate or adherent of moral legalism.
2. One that views things from a legal standpoint, especially one that places primary emphasis on legal principles or on the form of governmental institutions. Legalistic/adjective; legalistically/ adverb [284]

Here are some descriptions of legalism: As Manser, sees it, the belief that salvation demands or depends upon total obedience to the letter of the law. "Examples include an excessive concern for minute

---

[282] John MacArthur, *Expository Preaching* (Dallas TX: Word Publishing, 1992).

[283] John William Drane, *Introducing the Old Testament*, completely revised and updated (Oxford: Lion Publishing, 2000), 342.

[284] Merriam-Webster, *Merriam-Webster's Collegiate Dictionary*, 11*th* ed. (Springfield, MA: Merriam-Webster, 2003).

details of the law coupled with a neglect of its fundamental concerns, and a preoccupation with human legal traditions."[285] He then goes on to list some of those things:

1. Legalism represents a fatal misunderstanding of the purpose of OT law (Rom 3:20, 9:31–32; Gal 3:10–11).
2. Legalism is contrary to the gospel (Gal 2:16, Mt 23:13–15, Rom 3:20–24, Phil 3:8–9).
3. Paul was an example of a Jewish legalist (Phil 3:4–6, Gal 1:14).
4. The ugly effects of legalism are a lack of love and disregard for the concerns of people (Mt 23:23).
5. Legalism actually contradicts the spirit of Old Testament law (Hos 6:6, Mi 6:7–8, Mt 23:14, Lk 10:31–32, Jn 7:49).
6. Legalism causes spiritual pride and arrogance (Lk 18:9–14; Mt 6:1–2, 5, 16, 23:5–7; Lk 16:15; Rom 10:3).
7. Legalism leads to formalism (Is 29:13, Mk 7:6).
8. It degenerates into man-made rules (Is 29:13, Mk 7:7–8).
9. It creates hypocrisy (Mt 23:27–28, 1 Sm 15:19–22, Mt 15:3, Mk 7:9–13, Mt 23:25–26, Jn 7:19).
10. It causes spiritual blindness (Jn 9:16).
11. Warnings against legalism are given (Mt 16:6, 12; Mk 8:15; Gal 4:10–11, 5:2–4).
12. It is a burden and brings bondage (Acts 15:10, Ps 130:3, Jas 2:10).
13. The answer to legalism is the grace of Jesus (Acts 15:11; Mt 5:17; Gal 3:13, 4:21–31; Eph 2:8–10.)[286]

So, we can begin to understand what Paul was dealing with. It wasn't that someone just hurt someone else's feelings. Nor were

---

[285] Martin H. Manser, *Dictionary of Bible Themes: The Accessible and Comprehensive Tool for Topical Studies* (London: Martin Manser, 2009), Logos.

[286] Ibid.

EQUIPPED FOR HOLINESS

these Christians just trying to live in the Spirit rather than the flesh. This was a much bigger problem. These men who had come from Jerusalem wanted to put these people back under the bondage of Judaism—to try to convince them that they had to earn their salvation by works, even to the point of mutilating their bodies in circumcision. To do so makes void the sacrifice of Christ (Heb 6:4–6). These men were not trying to help these people lead a more godly life. They were trying to enslave them. Dockery points out that even in Colossae, where the men were not free from the circumcision, the Judaizers were at work trying to do the very same thing to them as they were doing in Galatia.[287]

We live in this physical world, yet John tells (Jn 17:15–16) that Jesus prayed for us to be kept from the evil one and be sanctified by the truth. That truth is His Word. Paul says when we were saved we were translated from the power of darkness into God's kingdom (Col 1:13). As a result we should govern our lives by His laws rather than man's. Wiersbe would remind us that this is not to suggest that we are to be lawless. Rather, we should always be respectful of those in authority (1 Pt 2:11; Rom 12, 13).[288]

This is the same type of problem that antinomianism presented, and it is a Christological error in that it deals with the atonement. As Ravi Zacharias said, "While Antinomianism and Legalism superficially appear to be opposites the reality is that they are the same, error."[289]

The Judaizers were telling the Galatians that belief in Christ to save them was not enough. Something more was required, which in this case was making men then responsible for their own salvation. This is adding to the work of Christ on the cross. While antinomianism teaches that Christ's work on the cross left nothing else to be done, implying that a Christian was free to live in any manner he or she

---

287 David S. Dockery, "The Pauline Letters" in Holman Concise Bible Commentary, ed. (Nashville, TN: Broadman & Holman, 1998), 591–93.
288 Wiersbe, Col 2:18, 3:11.
289 Ravi Zacharias, interview, YouTube.

137

chose without fear of any reprisals. Both were teaching a totally false gospel. Both were heresy then the same as they are now.

It might be noted that these Judaizers had an agenda; they weren't just Jewish Christians who were trying to live for Christ. Rather, they were deceivers and were out to wreak havoc in the church, bringing in man-made laws to the Gentiles who were swarming to Christ.

Tan explains that the law was never capable of giving life or being fruitful because it was barren. If the fledgling church were to go back under the bondage of the law it too would become barren—becoming disobedient to the Word of God. Because of the early church's faithfulness and steadfastness to the message of grace, preached by Paul, it spread exponentially in fruitfulness.[290]

According to Wiersbe there wasn't a whole lot of doubt that the Judaizers were attractive people. They carried all the right credentials from the religious authorities (2 Cor 3:1). They had high standards and were very careful in what they ate and drank. They were good at making converts and liked to advertise their accomplishments (Gal 4:17–18, 6:12–14). They had rules and standards to cover every area of life, making it easy for their followers to know who was "spiritual" and who wasn't. Nonetheless, the Judaizers were leading the people into bondage and defeat, not the liberty and victory of the gospel, but the Galatians weren't sharp enough or knowledgeable enough to recognize the difference.[291]

The Judaizers accused Paul of teaching a dangerous doctrine of grace where the Gentiles would have license to sin, claiming that he was teaching them to ignore their rules and regulations. They reasoned that by abandoning their high standards the church would fall apart as a result. Were they accusing Paul of preaching antinomianism? Paul was quick to remedy this little

---

[290] Paul Lee Tan, *Encyclopedia of 7700 Illustrations: Signs of the Times* (Garland, TX: Bible Communications, 1996), 725.

[291] Warren W. Wiersbe, *The Bible Exposition Commentary*, Gal 4:30–32, Logos.

misunderstanding in the final section of his letter (in Gal 5:6). Paul's doctrine was not teaching antinomianism, as his doctrine consisted of Christian liberty through grace, and there was nothing dangerous about it.

Weirsbe says that the surrendered Christian who depends on the power of the Spirit is not denying the law of God; nor are they rebelling against it. They understand that the law is being fulfilled in them through the power of the Spirit (Rom 8:1–4). Scripture bears this out:

1. Galatians 5:20 says, I have been set free by Christ, I am no longer under the bondage to the Law. To go back under the law is to fall from grace.
2. Galatians 5:13–26 says, the Holy Spirit controls my life from within.
3. Galatians 6:1–10 says, through the Spirit's love, I want to live for others, not myself.
4. Galatians 6:11–18 says, this life of liberty is so wonderful, I want to live it to the glory of God; for He is the One making it possible.[292]

Conclusion

Legalism is an outward religion without an inward work of the Spirit. It is a shell without an inner life. It is empty, lifeless, just rote behavior. By obeying the laws and regulations of whatever cult, sect, or group leader one can only hope to achieve salvation. While struggling with thoughts like these, totally without any type of assurance. According to Weirsbe:

---

[292] Ibid. Weirsbe

- If I obey these rules and do what they say, I will become more spiritual. I am a great admirer of this religious leader or group, so I strive to submit to their system.
- I believe I have the strength to obey and improve myself. I do what I am told and measure up to the standards that are set for me.
- I am making progress. I don't do some of the things I used to do. Others compliment me on my obedience and discipline. I can see that I am better than others in my fellowship. How wonderful it is to be so spiritual.
- If only others were more like me. God is so fortunate that I am His. I have a desire to share this with others so they can be as I am. Our group is growing, and we have a fine reputation. Too bad other groups are not as spiritual as we are.[293]

Is this what the scriptures would teach us? Of course not. We have been saved and set free from the law by the blood of Jesus Christ. We are no longer in bondage to it. Legalism breeds pride and arrogance; Christians are set free from the law to be able to fulfill it. Not by our own power, as we are powerless to do it, but by God's unending grace and the power of His Holy Spirit—no longer to follow rules and regulations but to walk in the relationship of His love. What a joy and privilege God has given His children.

Pride is the attitude of the legalist not some common ordinary Christian trying his best to serve his Lord in humility and humble service, fully appreciating all the while that he can never do this under his own power and recognizing his only hope is to lean on the Holy Spirit to take him through. No, the legalist is a horse of a completely different color, and there is no comparison between the two. Wiersbe describes "legalism as an insidious, dangerous enemy."

---

[293] Ibid. Weirsbe

In Galatians 5:1–12, Paul explains what happens when a believer turns from God's grace to man's rules and regulations.[294]

Wiersbe goes on to point out that to the New Testament Christian, obedience is a practice of "good deeds, performed by those who are already redeemed by the blood of Jesus." We are to be rich in good deeds (1 Tm 6:18; Mt 5:16; Eph 2:10; 2 Tm 3:17; Ti 2:7, 14, 3:8, 14). A good deed is one done according to the right standard (God's revealed will—His moral law).[295] Also it should be as a result of a right motive (loving God and others that speaks of a regenerate heart). Then it should be with a right purpose (pleasing and glorifying God, honoring Christ and advancing His kingdom, and benefiting one's neighbor).

Legalism is a distortion of the truth of the Bible and can never produce good works. First, because its motives are skewed. The legalist sees good deeds as a way to earn His salvation. Second, the legalist becomes arrogant and has contempt for anyone who does not do as he does. Third, this in turn causes lovelessness within the legalist. The Judaizers of Paul's day were the Jesus Plus Movement.[296] It was okay to believe in Jesus so long as you did all the other things a good Jew would do. That is what sets this apart as another gospel, different from the one Paul preached. It added to the work of Christ. Not only did it add to the simplicity of the gospel, it bound them back up in the same bondage that Jesus's death and resurrection freed them from.

Nowadays whenever someone screams "legalist," we need to take a long look at what they are really saying. Just because people may be trying their best to please God does not make them legalists unless they declare it is necessary for their salvation. Let us understand that the Judaizers of Paul's day were there to deceive and destroy the work that had begun among the Gentiles. They had an agenda.

---

[294] Warren H. Wiersbe, *The Bible Exposition Commentary*, Gal 5:1–26.

[295] Ibid. Weirsbe.

[296] J. I. Packer, *Concise Theology: A Guide to Historic Christian Beliefs*, 175–77.

As Christians, we need to take a look at ourselves and see if any of these things ring our bell, as maybe we have taken on the persona of the legalist.

So often legalism can just slip in unnoticed and totally unintentional. Maybe that is what makes it so insidious and dangerous to us. Possibly in our zeal to win over others or find favor with God, we have mistakenly stepped over into a legalistic mind frame. If this is the case, let us quickly renounce it and ask for forgiveness and let God cleanse us from a legalistic attitude. It is very easy to come by. We want to walk in purity and love being led by the Spirit of God. Not just for ourselves so much as a need to want to reach others with the good news of the gospel. That good news is that God has delivered us from such bondage, and we can all be free in Him. Free to do what? Free to live for Him, which we can never do under the bondage of legalism. Where the Spirit of the Lord is, there is freedom (2 Cor 3:17).

10

CHAPTER

Tying It All Together

Well, here we are just about to end our quest for holiness. Or maybe it is just the beginning of a lifelong quest in a new believer. Whatever the case, one will never regret moving toward holiness in his or her life and walk with the Lord. The point is, and this is really good news, as believers we have nothing to lose and everything to gain by seeking after holiness. Can the same be said if we choose not to follow in Christ's footsteps? It is our choice.

There is so much more to be said on the subject and why it is of such importance to the believer, but we merely want to do a recap and touch on the highlights. What is this thing called holiness? What is its importance, and what on earth does it look like? Hopefully, some of these questions have been answered.

We must understand that there is no holiness apart from the Holy Spirit. He is the one who produces holiness from within us. Anything else is legalism. Our job is simply to respond to the leading of the Spirit in accordance with His Word. He has changed us and is still changing us. Why would we ever want to get stuck where we were? Or for that matter, go back to it? Jesus's death and resurrection broke the chains that bound us. What person, having had his or her chains of bondage broken would pick them up and put them back on? No one in his or her right mind. So it is with the Christian. We have been set free by the blood of Jesus Christ—freedom to walk on in that freedom. When a bird is freed from its cage (or bondage) it is free to fly, and it is expected do so. This is a freedom like no other. It is not the freedom to go on sinning. No, this is a real freedom to walk in the Spirit. The choice is ours.

In the real world it takes a long time to grow fruit. The same thing can be said of our spiritual lives too. Fruit does not grow overnight. It takes a lifetime. It is interesting that when asked how we would know the real Christians from the false, the Bible says it would be by their fruit that we would know them. Not by their looks or how they dressed. Not by how much they knew about the Bible. Not even by special gifts they may possess. But simply by the fruit being produced in their lives. Namely, if it is good fruit it is from God. If it is bad fruit it is not. This is how holiness displays itself, through the beautiful fruit of the Spirit.

We have journeyed through the fundamentals of the faith—of sin and its origin—in chapter 1. What it means to repent and why it is necessary for salvation. God's great plan for the salvation of man and how He Himself put it into place and carried it through.

In chapter 2 we learned about God's character, especially in regard to His holiness. There is so much more that could be written regarding His character and attributes. Unfortunately, it would take us a thousand lifetimes to do so, and then we would merely scratch the surface. That's because the nature and character of God is unfathomable.

We learned in chapter 3 of our need as Christians to be holy and what that entails. It is not just walking around with a holier than thou expression, following a lot of man-made rules, regulations, and traditions while looking down on those less enlightened than them. It is something that goes much deeper than appearances. They say that ugly goes clear to the bone. Well, holiness goes straight through the heart, changing our minds, attitudes, actions, and responses in the process.

We touched on the deity of Christ in chapter 4. Again, that is another topic that could take many lifetimes to get a good rendering or comprehension of. Hopefully we have gained a little better appreciation of why this is of such great importance in our lives. When we are able to grasp the correct picture of who Jesus really is, it changes our outlook and focus forever, helping us to direct our attention to the author and finisher of our faith, the Lord Jesus Christ (Heb 12:2).

We have seen the need of and the importance of obedience in the believer's life in chapter 5. Then we crossed over the rugged terrain of grace and holiness in chapter 6 to discover how it is that they work together to bring about fullness in the life of a believer. That was followed closely by the law and the gospel in chapter 7, paying close attention to how the two are not only compatible but intertwine like a beautiful tapestry, bringing about God's will not only in the life of believers but for the world at large.

From there we took a peek at two of the main antagonists of holiness down through the ages—antinomianism in chapter 8 and legalism in chapter 9—and how these two heresies affect us even today.

In chapter 8 we learned that antinomianism, although very old in origin, is alive and well and making headway in the church today, with its liberal teachings on grace. It is an ancient heresy all dressed up in the garb of hypergrace, radical grace, or in some circles known as greasy grace. This is not the gospel of Jesus Christ anymore than legalism is.

We learned in chapter 9 that God's holiness changes us from the inside out, whereas hollow religion seeks to change people from the outside in. Holiness is not just behavior modification. Holiness is a change of nature, character, and spirit. The Holy Spirit is the one who starts the changes from within and works through to the outside. This is the change we want in our lives—God working through us for His honor and glory.

Jerry Iwaarden explains it like this:

> Man, was created in God's image is also said to be a triune being. The body which encompasses the flesh, the soul which is the seat of our emotions, feelings, and experiences. Then there is the Spirit which is the domain of our innermost being. This is where we either belong to the kingdom of darkness or the kingdom of light. This is where we once lived in darkness controlled by our sin and our flesh.[297]

Now that those sins have been forgiven, by the blood of Jesus Christ, we are no longer ruled by our lower nature. Instead we are now governed by His Holy Spirit. We are or should be ruled by His righteousness, as opposed to our flesh. We have been changed, and we are being changed (Col 1:10–13).

Thus as we tie this study up, maybe we can look at holiness in a new light, forming a new perspective on the subject. Not as something to be avoided at all cost, but rather something to be pursued and embraced with a passion. Many Christians can remember the days when the holiness group was made up of the kids at school that could not take part in after-school functions because they were "sinful"—dancing, going to a movie, not being allowed to wear makeup or listen to rock and roll on the radio. Where every week the deacons and elders and rest of the adults in church were rushing to the altar to be saved, again, simply because of some evil deed they had done, or thought of doing, during the week. Well, this is not the holiness of which we are speaking.

Quite often in the past people were judged to be Christians or not based on outward appearances. If they smoked cigarettes, it was

---

[297] Pastor Jerry Van Iwaarden, private interview, June 28, 2018, pastor, Westview Assembly of God, Cedar City, UT.

said that other Christians were not to assume it was because "they were on fire for the Lord." If they had an occasional drink it was taken for granted that they knew they were on their way to perdition. Women didn't have babies without husbands; it just wasn't heard of. But then every woman had a husband. It wasn't all bad, though, as almost every child had a mother and father. A respectable woman didn't wear pants in public, and a man didn't have long hair. Tattoos were disgraceful and covered up, certainly not flaunted. Only the heathen had piercings. These were the types of things Christians were judged by—all outward manifestations. These definitely were not signs of the Holy Spirit residing within.

Yes, these were legalistic things, while believers are told in the scripture not to judge folks by the outside. God is the judge, and He judges people from the inside, where it counts (1 Sm 16:7). Yet because people are human, they still do. It should be pointed out it wasn't just holiness groups that judged this way; most other Christian groups did as well. The difference in the holiness group and the Baptist is that it was okay if the Baptists did these things. Who was right and who was wrong? Maybe neither; maybe both. In their exuberance, maybe the holiness tribe just overreacted by resorting to man-made rules and regulations.

Could be the Baptists just needed a little stronger boundaries. Scripture is very plain as to what sin is. We just need to steer clear of it. Yes, we have boundaries as Christians. These boundaries are for our good; they are not to hurt us. Many of these church-made rules, regulations, and traditions were hard things imposed upon believers. No doubt good intentions were at the base of many of these. However, it still leads us into bondage, where a person's salvation is judged not on his or her relationship with the Lord but on outward signs, where it then becomes a substandard assessment by any standard.

Why do people put up fences around their property? To protect what is inside from escaping and getting hurt or killed (namely children, pets, and livestock). Also, it is a barrier to keep harmful things away (such as wolves, wild beasts, and bad dudes). It is done to protect possessions and loved ones. As Cloud and Townsend say, "boundaries are put up to keep the good in and the bad out."[298] We put them up for a reason. It's because these things are precious to us.

God has also set boundaries for His children. Why? Because we are precious to Him. He doesn't want us hurt or destroyed. Christians are safe within the parameters God has set for them, if they abide within those boundaries (Jn 15:4). It is when one deliberately wanders beyond them that they open themselves up for harm and bondage in their lives.

What is true in nature is also true in the spiritual realm. Wolves and lions along with other predators normally do not attack the herd. They wait and watch for the weak and sickly ones, who cannot keep up. Or they wait patiently for a young one to wander off from the safety of the others. It is when one separates himself or herself from the boundaries of the herd that he or she becomes vulnerable. The group itself is a boundary for each member of the herd, to protect and to keep all of them safe. It is when some take their eyes off the flock or decide they know more than the rest or see some tantalizing sight and run after it that they put themselves in danger. The same is true of our Christian walk. We need to understand that God has put up the boundaries, and we should remain within them for our own safety as well as the safety of the rest of the group. The fact that God has set these boundaries for us proves His love and concern for our welfare.

After all, Jesus died to set the believer free, so the least one can do is comply with His standard, living within the blessed freedom He has bestowed. Paul would sum it up this way: "It is for freedom that Christ has set us free. Stand Firm, do not let yourselves be burdened again by the yoke of slavery" (Gal 5:1 NIV). Not always

---

[298]   Dr. Henry Cloud and Dr. John Townsend, *Boundaries* (Grand Rapids, MI: Zondervan, 2017), location 716.

looking and longing for the proverbial greener pasture on the other side of the fence.

Even so, holiness is still so much more than this. It is first and foremost a relationship with a Holy God, and it is a relationship based on love. It is because we love Him that we no longer desire to do things that might displease Him. It is our motivation that is important. It is because we love Him and desire to please Him, not that we have to do this or else. We make mistakes, and we fall down. It is then that we look up and realize that we are free, and He has made provision for us, so that in the event we do sin, it does not mean we are lost or cast aside. All we have to do is confess that sin for what it is, turn away, and keep on moving forward.

This is freedom, knowing that He loves us and wants us to have the victory over these things that would entangle us. So we live, not in a fearful state of a wrathful God who is just waiting for us to make a mistake so He can whip out His cosmic flyswatter and clobber us. On the contrary, He is the loving Father who longs to pick us up, dust us off, encourages us to do better, and then sends us back on our way. Cloud and Townsend also point out that God is very specific about what He allows to enter into His yard. He actively confronts sin while allowing us to face the consequences for our behavior. He desires that we would be responsible for the life with which He has blessed us.[299] When we do, we can live our lives with joy, peace, and contentment knowing that He wants us to have an abundant life in Him (Jn 10:10).

Okay, let's think about what holiness looks like or should look like in the life of a believer. We don't need to go any further than the fruit of the Spirit. John Owens would tell us that the fruit of the Spirit is a direct result of the Holy Spirit working in and through us. It is nothing we have done of ourselves.[300] Here are the works of the Holy Spirit living within us producing the fruit of the Spirit—the fruit

---

[299]   Ibid, Cloud & Townsend, location 725.
[300]   John Owens, *The Holy Spirit*, (Carlisle, PA: Banner of Truth, 1965), 476.

being love, joy, peace, patience, kindness, goodness, faithfulness, gentleness, and self control (Gal 5:22). This is as opposed to the works of the flesh (Gal 5:19–21)—sexual immorality, impurity, and debauchery; idolatry and witchcraft; hatred, discord, jealousy, fits of rage, selfish ambition, dissensions, factions and envy; drunkenness, orgies, and the like. What a contrast. Zornes mentions that Paul's list is not exhaustive and that the works of the flesh could be aptly termed the fruit of the flesh.[301] Therefore it could be pointed out that we are going to produce fruit in our lives whether good or bad. Let us make wise choices as Christians.

We can see from these two groups that the fruit of the Spirit is very attractive and draws unbelievers to the Lord. Bridges would point out that other traits could be added to the list of fruit as well. Including a humble and forgiving heart, one given to hospitality and compassion, integrity, contentment, a grateful or thankful heart, full of joy, perserverance and again humility.[302]

One other important element besides the fruit is humility. Holiness is humility in action, and from this humility comes forth fruit. Pride and arrogance have no place in the Christian life. Who did Jesus say was going to inherit the earth? The mighty and proud or the meek? Meekness is not weakness, because humility is not weakness. It is strength under willful submission, and it is a beautiful thing. Now let us take a quick look at the fruit again: love, joy, peace, faithfulness, goodness, gentleness, kindness, patience, self-control. What does this mean to us?

All of our effort to produce this fruit will not do it. The fruit is simply a by-product of the Holy Spirit working in our lives. As we grow and mature in Christ the fruit is being produced. Bridges would again add that "Christian character arises from our active

---

[301] Ben Zornes, *The Fruitful Life: Meditations on the Fruit of the Spirit* (Windsor, CO: Ellerslie Press), location 44, Kindle.

[302] Ibid, Jerry Bridges. The Fruitful Life (Colorado Springs, Co: NavPress, 2006) Kindle, Ed.

involvement in and with the divine nature (2 Pt 1:4) and is therefore a work of the Spirit," not a result of work on our part.[303]

What exactly does holiness look like? How would one identify it, if he or she ran right smack dab into it? Is it merely an attitude? There is attitude involved, yet so much more than that. The fruit of the Spirit would probably be the best way to describe the working of the Holy Spirit within a believer. The fruit is definitely signs of God working in a person's life. It isn't just the words of one's mouth, although that is very important. Nor is it just the visible signs of the Spirit or the supernatural gifts of the Spirit (1 Cor 12–14). This is not to minimize the importance of these things but rather just to put them in their proper perspective. Sinclair Ferguson says that the gifts of the Spirit mentioned in 1 Corinthians 12 should not be confused with the fruit mentioned in Galatians 5:22–23. They are separate. He goes on to say that although they are different, they should not be separated either; we should just know the difference. If there is no love or humility, the whole purpose of the gifts would be destroyed, giving the wrong motive for the gifts of the Spirit.[304] Once again although the two—the gifts and the fruit of the Spirit—are different, they do not operate independently from one another; 1 Corinthians 13 makes this abundantly clear.

The fruit of the Spirit is love, joy, peace, patience, kindness, goodness, faith, gentleness, and self-control. All of these articulate the transforming power of the Holy Spirit in a believer's life (Gal 5:22–23). These speak of holiness at work. When we walk in the Spirit rather than the flesh this then becomes holiness in action (Jn 15:1–5).

Let's take a quick look at the works of the flesh and those things that should not be evident in a believer's life. Galatians 5: 19–21 states "that the works of the flesh are obvious: sexual immorality,

---

[303]   Ibid. Bridges, 177.

[304]   Sinclair Ferguson, *The Holy Spirit* (Downers Grove, IL: InterVarsity, 1997), 209.

moral impurity, promiscuity, idolatry, sorcery, hatreds, strife, jealousy, outbursts of anger, selfish ambitions, dissensions, factions, envy, drunkenness, carousing, and anything similar." Paul explains to them that the Spirit is against the flesh, that they are opposed to each other, and that if a person is led by the Spirit then they are no longer under the law (vv. 16–18).

When Paul lists the fruit of the Spirit he says very plainly that there is no law against these things (v. 23). One who belongs to Christ Jesus crucifies the flesh with its passions and desires. We will be able to identify those false teachers by their fruit (Mt 7:15–20). Jesus said a good tree produces good fruit, and so will a bad tree produce bad fruit. He went on to say that a good tree couldn't produce bad fruit, just as a bad tree could not produce good fruit. This is how believers would know false teachers—by their lack of good fruit. This is not to give Christians license to be fruit inspectors, but when a person confesses Christ, there should be some sign of the presence of godly fruit. Granted it may be early fruit not yet ripened, but there should be evidence of fruit even if it is just tiny blossoms. Fruit takes a long time to come to fruition. It doesn't happen overnight in the natural world; nor should one expect it to in the spiritual world.

Along about this time it should be pointed out that the fruit of the Spirit is not grown by a person's own effort. One cannot produce this fruit on his or her own. It is a by-product of the Holy Spirit residing within a person. People may have a certain amount of ability whereby they may be able to change their minds and maybe their behavior and do better, but this is not what is being referred to here. The work and fruit of the Spirit is produced from within. Christians can participate and help cultivate this fruit by spending time in His Word: through prayer in communion and intimate communication with Him, followed by taking time to fellowship with other believers. All of these things help one grow and mature in Him as he or she is being transformed (Rom 12:1–2). However, the fruit itself is the result of the Holy Spirit working within a person, not due to his or her own efforts.

Some Christians think that since they have the Bible, they no longer have a need of the Holy Spirit to lead them to holiness. This too is legalism and wrong thinking. Trying to be holy without the help of the Holy Spirit is trying to be holy by one's own effort. Holiness can never be aside from the Holy Spirit. If we do this on our own, it produces dead religion, as opposed to life in the Spirit if we can just remember that the Holy Spirit and the Word never disagree. If the Spirit is disagreeing with the Word, we have the wrong spirit.

Therefore if we want to know what holiness looks like, look no further than the fruit of the Spirit (Gal 5). In 1 Corinthians 13, Paul says that even if we have experienced all the gifts of the Spirit, if we do not have love we are deceiving ourselves. Love is the greatest of the gifts, itself being one of the fruits of the Spirit. Holiness is always motivated by the love of God and love for not only His people but everyone. Our God is a loving God, and He loves people. Therefore it only stands to reason that as Christians we too should love or try to love people as God does and learn to see them through His eyes. After all it is while we were yet sinners that Christ died for us (Rom 5:8).

Know that holiness is something beautiful, wonderful, and of such great value, as opposed to something fearful, burdensome, or to be avoided at all cost. Here is another thought: holiness never makes us ashamed or makes us feel defeated. Unholy behavior does. We might want to take a closer look and realize that holiness is a place of freedom for the child of God, not some restrictive thing meant to steal all of our joy. That freedom in Christ should be the pursuit of our hearts for more of Him and less of ourselves. John 10:10 says that Jesus came to give us life and life more abundantly, and that is what holiness is. It is not a list of things meant to deprive us of joy; it is indeed what gives us joy.[305]

---

[305] Bryan Chappell, *Holiness by Grace: Delighting in the Joy That Is Our Strength* (Wheaton IL: Crossway Books, 2001).

The joy of the Lord is our strength says Nehemiah 8:10. Wait! Isn't joy one of the fruits of the Spirit? Then why are so many Christians lacking in joy today? Again, as has been stated earlier, God did not save us to make us happy; He saved us to make us holy. But He did promise to fill us with His joy. Weirsby again points out that many confuse happiness with joy, but they are not the same. Happiness is ruled by our emotions and circumstances and can change in a heartbeat.[306] Joy is everlasting and springs up from within even in the darkest of times. He has given us this joy, and the way we experience it is through living in the Spirit, rather than the flesh (Gal 5:16–17).

These are vexing problems today; we have a culture that is becoming more perverse and violent, seeking pleasure all the time and at any cost. Many would claim their Christianity amidst their perverseness. The problem now is that we are seeing these things not only in the world around us but tolerated within the churches and in many cases proclaimed from the pulpit. Where in the scripture does it say that we can be a Christian and continue in the same sin that brought us to our knees in the first place? It doesn't. This teaching does not ring true, and upon hearing this teaching our baloney alarms should immediately start to go off. Shame on us if we teach such a thing.

Eugene Peterson explains that there are millions of folks who make decisions for Christ, but that rate falls away dramatically.[307] He clarifies by saying that they just don't grow in maturity. While there is a big market for religious experience, there is very little patience for seeking virtue and purity, with very little desire to sign up for the long haul. Namely what older generations called "holiness."[308]

---

[306] Warren W. Wiersbe, *Be Holy*, "Be" Commentary Series (Wheaton, IL: Victor Books, 1996), 9.

[307] Eugene Peterson, *A Long Obedience in the Same Direction* (Downers Grove, IL: InterVarsity Press), Kindle location 194.

[308] Ibid., Kindle location 204.

One has to wonder sometimes whether the sacred-secular split that we hear so much about today hasn't just given way to the secular views, the way it is invading the churches.[309] Our culture in the last few decades has taken a decided turn in its worldviews. What once was taken for granted as to their being a created universe and orderly design by a loving, caring God has given way to myths of science along with Darwin's theory of evolution. This worldview is now operating in some churches without restraint, along with pressure from LGBQT groups nationally, the breakdown of the family, the rise of the feminist agenda, and a spirit of lawlessness that is invading our country (1 Jn 3:4). It would appear that the church is under attack. The gospel has been watered down in all areas when it should be proclaiming the truth of scripture. There should be a call back to holiness. Not legalism, for that is not true Christianity, but holiness, humility, and all the fruit of the spirit of Christ.

We can begin to see a need for a new take on holiness. Why do we need it? Well, we certainly are mandated to tell of the Good News of the Gospel and what Jesus has done for us.[310] These things are coming upon our country like a flood of filth. Still, the Bible says when "the enemy comes in like a flood, God's Spirit will raise up a standard against it" (Is 59:19). What is that standard? Truth, holiness, justice, righteousness? As Christians who love God we want the witness of a holy life to back up our testimonies lest we bring ridicule on the name of Jesus. A holy life bears witness to what we are saying. A holy life brings honor and glory to God.

Not everyone is called to be a pastor or an evangelist, but every blood-washed person is called to bring glory to God. How do we do this? By submitting to God and His Word. Submitting ourselves to do whatever His Word tells us we should do. By bending the knee in humble obedience to the one who is now our master. We have been bought with a price that was far above that of bulls and goats (Heb

---

[309] Nancy Pearson, *Total Truth* (Wheaton, IL: Crossway Books, 2005), 23.
[310] Pearson.

9:11–15). We belong to Him, and we need to start acting like it. A slave would not bring dishonor on his master. It was a disgraceful thing to bring dishonor to one's master, and they paid the price for such disobedience in the flesh and more often than not publicly.

The Bible makes it clear that in Christ we now have freedom to walk away and leave behind the sins from which we were forgiven. But what about those pet sins we keep around, such as anger, jealousy, conceit, envy, and legalism, which we pull out every now and then at our convenience. By God's glorious grace we are now free to walk beyond that with assurance of victory over them too (Rom 6:1). Those little sins sneak in just like the little foxes that spoil the vine of which Solomon spoke (Sg 2:15). Sometimes we are so intent on steering clear of the big sins that these little ones just sneak right in unannounced and uninvited. As Christians, we need to guard our hearts.

This is something to shout about; just to think of it should bring such intense joy into our lives as to change us completely from what we once were—sinners. We are no longer sinners saved by grace (although we certainly still sin); God calls us His saints because we have been changed and regenerated by the Holy Spirit, who has taken up residence within us. Not just saints, but saints of the Most High God. Almost scary to think about, but think about it we must.

We have the power of almighty God living within us. How do we explain it? We cannot, for words fail us; only God knows the answer to that one. Yet we by His mercy are the recipients of such grace. He has washed our sins away, by His very own blood, and set His Holy Spirit inside of us.

Why, then, would we ever want to continue on as a sinner? We have been saved, redeemed, and filled with His very own Spirit. We are no longer just sinners saved by grace; we are the redeemed of the Lord, and even though we still sin (the residue of that sinful nature still resides within us), it is not the same as willfully disobeying God. It is just a shortcoming on our part—the fact that we are still human and fall short of His glory (Rom 3:23), as opposed to an actual outward rebellion on our part.

He has given us the victory, and its time the church took up that banner once again of holiness. The banner seems to have fallen into the dust and needs to be picked up once again—not only a new awareness of the holiness of God but true holiness unto God. It's that important. The Bible says without holiness no man shall see the Lord (Heb 12:14). It is a worthy undertaking, as Paul said, to walk worthy of that vocation to which we were called (Eph 4:1). The blessings of obedience are for us.

In our churches today we hear so much about passion in our relationship with Christ. And this at a time when so many of our churches seem to be dead shells of something that used to be very much alive. We need the Holy Spirit more than ever. When we are born again, and God's Spirit comes to make His home within us, we are changed. Paul says that the old things are passed away, and everything is new (2 Cor 5:17). This is a wonderful example of what takes place at our conversion. Every Christian should be filled with passion for Christ. Not just a passion that deals with feelings and emotions that we often mistake for God's presence, but a real life-changing enthusiasm for the things of God. We want to serve and please Him. We are grateful for everything He has done and is doing for us. We are so thankful for the grace He has bestowed upon us, especially when we realize that we did not deserve it, that we want not just to bask in His glory and presence but dedicate every fiber of our being to Him. That is the essence of holiness. We no longer desire to be our own; we willingly submit to His authority, and this in return brings us great joy and blessing and peace (1 Thes 4:1–8). Obedience to God has its own rewards, and they are far above anything this world has to offer (1 Cor 2:9).

Does this mean we will never have another financial need, or physical or emotional need, or never succumb to temptation, or that disease might never ravage our bodies? Of course not; what it does mean is we can rest assured knowing that God is in control of every area of our lives, and nothing can separate us from Him except our own rebellion (Rom 8:35). We would have to work really hard to even make that a possibility. Christians should not be defiant by living in sin while expecting the blessings of God in their lives. We should seek to ferret out those things that the Holy Spirit reveals to us that are not pleasing to God. This is sanctification in action.

We all sin and fall short of God's glory; that isn't the sin of which we speak. We are talking about that habitual sin (or a pet sin) that we are unwilling to give up, or knowing full well something is sin and doing it anyway in defiance of God's word (1 Jn 5:17). We can never be perfect; nor should we try. God hasn't called us to perfection but to holiness.[311] But we can revel in the fact that God does make it possible for us to overcome sin in our lives. It can be noted that the things we allow in our own lives directly affect the church. Do we want to invite fornication, adultery, or other perversions of God's plan into our churches or homes? How about drunkenness or addictions? Then there are the petty ones such as lying, stealing, gossiping, bearing false witness, unforgiveness, bitterness, revenge, grumbling, backbiting, or being a busy body. Every one of which can be just as destructive. What is sin?

It is anything contrary to or falling short of the person, nature, and character of God. These things need to be rebuked, confessed, and abandoned.

We are the church, and Jesus is coming for us—His church or bride—and it is to be a church or bride without spot or blemish. Spurgeon had this to say concerning an unholy church. "On Sunday morning, January 24, 1861, Spurgeon closed his sermon at the Metropolitan Tabernacle with these words:

> An unholy Church! It is of no use to the world, and
> of no esteem among men. Oh, it is an abomination,
> hell's laughter, heaven's abhorrence. And the larger

---

[311] Charles Spurgeon, *Holiness Demanded*, www://http.puritandownloads.com.

the Church, the more influential, the worst nuisance does it become, when it becomes dead and unholy. The worst evils which have ever come upon the world, have been brought upon her by an unholy Church.[312]

A self-proclaiming Christian living an unholy life is not a pretty sight either. He or she can bring much shame and harm to the body of Christ. Jay Kesler tells us "there is nothing more damaging to the witness of the church than hypocritical leaders."[313] Our walk is just as important as our testimony. Possibly more so as more people see us than will ever hear us. As some people used to say, we may be (meaning our lives) the only Bible a person ever reads. If that is the case then how should we be conducting ourselves as Christians?

A person saying one thing while doing another causes mistrust. The message spoken does not ring true.

Zornes would bring to our attention that as Christians we are commanded throughout the Bible to bear fruit (Mt 3:8, Lk 3:8, Jn 15, Rom 7:4–5, Gal 5:22–23, Eph 5:9). Not by gritting our teeth and bearing down to produce, but simply by abiding in the vine.[314] The branches only have to stay connected to the vine in order to produce fruit worthy of salvation. It is only by staying connected to Jesus by means of the Holy Spirit. Jesus said He is the way, the truth, and the life. If we stay connected, it is safe to say that we cannot help but grow the fruit worthy of God's kingdom. This is what the Spirit produces in those who are called by His name.

Holiness is a beautiful thing. Real holiness draws people to God. God's holiness is so awesome that we humans cannot even

---

[312] Warren W. Wiersbe, *Be Holy*, "Be" Commentary Series (Wheaton, IL: Victor Books, 1996), 17.

[313] Jay Kesler, vol. 13, *Being Holy, Being Human: Dealing With the Expectations of Ministry*, Leadership Library (Carol Stream, IL, Waco, TX: Christianity Today, Word Books, 1988), 17–18.

[314] Zornes, Kindle location 44.

look upon Him face to face, lest we die (Ex 33:20). We need to start taking this seriously. Yet, Jesus was the visible image of the invisible God (Col 1:15). He alone has given us access through His death and resurrection to know Him.

Holiness is not something to shy away from; nor is it something that instills fear or panic in our hearts. Rather than fleeing from the mention of holiness as Christians, we should pursue it and embrace it fully. It is not burdensome but a delight for the believer. Holiness is a natural and spontaneous reaction to the presence of the Holy Spirit.

Let us not tread lightly on the magnificent grace and mercy God has shown us through the death and resurrection of His Son. No greater price has ever been paid. May we learn to treat it with the respect and honor this sacrifice deserves.

We now more than ever before have, through Christ, the ability to come before His presence with praise and thanksgiving. He was the means for His children to be made holy, and that is through His gift of grace to all believers. May we as believers make holiness our number one objective: to obey, trust, submit, to the only one true God. Why? Because we love Him. May all glory and honor be to God through our LORD Jesus Christ.

BIBLIOGRAPHY

Bibles cited

Amplified (AMP), 2015 by <u>The Lockman Foundation</u>, La Habra, CA 90631.

King James Version (KJV).

New International Version (NIV), 1973, 1978, 1984, 2011 by <u>Biblica, Inc.</u>® Used by permission. All rights reserved worldwide.

New King James Version (NKJV), 1982 by Thomas Nelson.

Bibliography

AkHimien, Solomon. *Is Jesus Christ God? A Concise Apology Satisfying the Gratuitous Dispute.* Kindle edition.

Anderson, Richard. *No Holiness, No Heaven.* Carlyle, PA: Banner of Truth Trust, 1986.

Arthur, Kay. NRB Broadcast, 1/28/16.

Aycock, Don M. *Living By the Fruit of the Spirit.* Grand Rapids, MI: Kegel Publications, 1999.

Barber, Cyril J. and Robert M. Krauss. *Introduction to Theological Research.* Lanham, MD: University Press, 2001.

Barnard, Rev. P. Mordant. *Early Church Classics: Vol 66: Volume 155: A Homely of Clement of Alexandria entitled: Who Is The Rich Man That Is Being Saved.* New York: E & J B. Young, 1901.

Bashan, Greg L. *The Theonomic Reformed Approach to Law and Gospel. Five Views of Law and Gospel.* Grand Rapids, MI: Zondervan, 1996.

Bavinck, Herman. *Reformed Dogmatics.* Grand Rapids, MI: Baker Academic, 2011.

Bevere, John. *A Heart Ablaze.* Nashville, TN: Thomas Nelson, 1999.

———. *Driven by Eternity: Make Your Life Count Today and Forever.* Palmer Lake, CO: Messenger International, 2016.

Bickle, Mike. "Introduction to Hypergrace." In *Hypergrace: Exposing the Danger of the Modern Grace Message*, by Dr. Michael Brown. Kindle Book.

Blomberg, Craig L. *Can We Still Believe the Bible?* Grand Rapids, MI: Bazos Press, 2014.

Bounds, Edward. *Power Through Prayer.* Oak Harbor, WA: Logos Research System, 199.

Bowker, John. *World Religions: The Great Faiths Explored & Explained.* New York: K. K. Publishing, 2006.

Bridges, Jerry. *The Fruitful Life.* Colorado Sprinss, Co: NavPress, 2004.

Brooks, Keith. *Summarized Bible: Complete Summary of the New Testament.* Bellingham WA: Logos Bible software, 2009.

Brooks, Thomas. *Precious Remedies Against Stan's Devices.* Kindle Books, 1608–80.

Brown, Dr. Michael. *Go and Sin No More.* Regal Books, 1999.

———. *Hypergrace:Exposing the Dangers of the Modern Grace Message.* Kindle, location 2022.

Bruce, F. F. *The Epistle to the Hebrews,* revised ed. Grand Rapids, MI: Eerdmens, 1990.

Butcher, James. *Christian Pharisees: The Striking Similarities of America's Conservative Christians and Jesus' Earthly Enemies.* Kindle edition.

Oden, C. Thomas. *Classic Christianity.* Broadway, NY: Harper Collins, 1992.

Cairns, Earle E. *Christianity through the Ages.* 3rd ed. Grand Rapids, MI: Zondervan, 1981.

Calvin, John. *Institutes of the Christian Religion.* Bellingham, WA: Logos Bible Software, 1997.

———. *Institutes of the Christian Religion II,* 3.6.5., p. 5.

———. *Institutes of the Christian Religion,* translated by Henry Beveridge. London: James Clark, 1949.

Campbell, Donald K. "Galatians." In *The Bible Knowledge Commentary: An Exposition of the Scriptures,* ed. J. F. Walvoord and R. B. Zuck, Gal 5:4–6. Wheaton, IL: Victor Books, 1985.

Campbell, Ian D. *Opening Up Exodus: Opening Up Commentary.* Leominster: Day One, 2006.

Chambers, Oswald. *My Utmost For His Highest: Selections for the Year.* Grand Rapids, MI: Oswald Chambers; Marshall Pickering, 1986.

———. *Biblical Ethics.* Hants UK: Marshall, Morgan & Scott, 1947.

———. *The Moral Foundation of Life: A Series of Talks on the Ethical Principle of the Christian Life.* Hants, UK: Marshall, Morgan & Scott, 1936.

Chapell, Bryant. *Holiness by Grace: Delighting in the Joy That Is Our Strenth.* Wheaton, IL: Crossway, 2001.

Cloud, Dr. Henry, and Dr. John Townsend. *Boundaries: When to Say Yes, How to Say No, to take Control of Your Life.* Grand Rapids, MI: Zondervan, 1992.

Cho, Dr. Paul Yonggi. *The Fourth Dimension.* Plainsfield, NJ: Logos.

Cocoris, Michael. *Repentance: The Most Misunderstood Word in the Bible.* Milwaukee, WI: Grace Publishing, 1982.

Comfort, Eugene E. Carpenter and Phillip W. Holman. *Treasury of Key Bible Words: 200 Greek and 200 Hebrew Words Defined and Explained.* Nashville, TN: Broadman & Holman, 2000.

Conway, Tim. *illbehonest.com*. 2017. http://illbehonest.com/ Holiness-of-God-Tim-Conway. (accessed 2017).

Copan, Paul. *Does the Moral Argument Show There Is a God? The Apologetics Study Bible: Real Questions, Straight Answers, Stonger Faith*, ed. Nashville, TN: Holman Bible Publishers, 2007.

Crutcher, Timothy J. *John Wesley: His Life and Thought*. Kansas City, MO; Beacon Hill. 2015.

Dallas, Joe. "Now What? Same Sex Marriage and Today's Church." *Christian Research Journal* ID:JAF6371.CRI.

Dockery, David S., Trent C. Butler, and Chistopher L. Church. *Holman Bible Handbook*. Nashville, TN: Holman Bible Publishers, Logos, 1992.

Davison, Marguerite Porter. *A Handweaver's Pattern Book,* revised ed. Davison, 1944.

Dieter, Melvin. *Five Views on Santification*. Grand Rapids, MI: Zondervan, 1987.

Diffenbaugh, Robert L. *God's Holiness*. 2016. http://bible.org/ servespage/5-holiness-god.

Dockery, David. "The Pauline Letters." In *Holman Concise Bible Commentary*, 591–93. Nashville, TN: Broadman and Holman, 1998.

Doyle, Sir Arthur Conan. *Sherlock Holmes: The Sign of the Four.* Double Day, 1890.

Dr. J. Ayodeji, Adwuya. *Transformed by Grace: Paul's View of Holiness in Romans 6–8*. Eugene, OR: Cascade Books, 2004.

Drane, John Willams. *Introducing The New Testament,* completely revised and updated. Oxford: Lion Publishing, 2000.

Dunning, Ray H. *Grace, Faith & Holiness*. Kansas City, MO: Beacon Hill, 1988.

Eckman. James P. *Exploring Church History*. Wheaton, IL: Crossway, 2002.

Edersheim, Alfred. *Sketches of Jewish Social Life*. New York: Hodder and Stoughton: George H. Doran, 1876.

Ellsworth, Roger. *Opening Up Joshua: Opening Up Commentary.* Leonminster: Day One Publication, 2008.

Ferguson, Sinclair Dr. "Law." *Table Talk, 17–24, June 2016*, vol. 40 *Ligoniers*, no. 6. Ligoniers Ministry.

———. *The Holy Spirit.* Downers Grove, IL: Intervarsity Press, 1997.

Fischer, John. *12 Steps for the Recovering Pharisee (like me): Finding Grace to Live Unmasked.* Minneapolis, MN: Bethany House,2000.

Fletcher, John. *The Words of John Fletcher.* Vol. 2. Schmull Reprings: Schmul Reprings, 1974.

Florida, Steve. *Spiritual Avalanche: The Threat of False Teachings That Could Destroy Millions.* Lake Mary,FLA: Charisma House, 2013.

Forsythe, Peter Taylor. *The Principles of Authority.* London: Haddor and Stoughton, 1912.

Frame, John M. *The Doctrine of the Word of God.* Phillipsburg, NJ: P & R Publishing, 2010.

Friel, Todd. Wretched TV. Directed by National Religious Broadcasting. Performed by Todd Friel, 2016.

Geisler, Norman L. "Colossians," *The Bible Knowledge Commentary.* Wheaton, IL: Victor Books, 1985.

Geisler, Norman L. and Roh Rhodes. *Correcting the Cults.* Grand Rapids, MI: Baker Books, 1997.

Gilkne, Langdon B. *Maker of Heaven and Earth.* Garden City, NY: Double Day, 1959.

Green, Randy. *Galatians Book III; Chapters 5–6. Voume 13 of Heavenly Citizens in Earthly Shoses: An Exposition of the Scriptures for Disciples and Young Christians.* Kindle ed., 2017.

Grudem, Wayne. *Bible Doctrine: Essential Teachings of the Christian Faith.* Grand Rapids, MI: Zondervan, 1999.

Guiness, Oz. *Impossible People.* Downers Grove: Intervarsity Press, 2016.

Hardin, Gary. "Obedience:" *Holman Illustrated Bible Dictionary,* ed. Nashville, TN: Holman Bible Publishers, 2003.

Hibbs, Jack. "Real Life with Jack Hibbs broadcast." Crossover Radio 88.9. Cedar City, UT, 2017.

Hick, John. *The Metaphor of God Incarnate.* Louisville, KY: Knox Press, 1993.

Hill, Steve. *Spiritual Avalanche.* Lake Mary, FL: Charisma Book, 2013.

Hobbs, Herschel H. *My Favorite Illustrations.* Nashville, TN: Broadman Press, 1990.

Hodges, A. A. *The Westminster Confession: A Commentary:* Chapter 8: Of Christ the Mediator; section P cii.

Hodges, Charles. *Systematic Theology.* Vol 3. Peabody, MA: Hendrickson, 2008.

Hoekema, Anthony A. *Five Views of Sanctification: Response to Dieter and the Wesleyan Perspective.* Grand Rapids, MI: Zondervan, 1987.

Horton, Stanley M. *Five Views of Sanctification: The Pentecostal Perspective.* Grand Rapids, MI: Zondervan, 1987.

Howard, Evan. "Three Temptations of Spiritual Formation." *Christianity Today* 46, no. 13, Dec. 9, 2002, 46.

Jones, Mark. *Antinomianism: Reformed Theology's Unwelcome Guest.* Phillipsburg, NJ: P & R Publishing, 2013.

Smith, Joseph Jr. "King Follett discourse." *Journal of Discovery* 6, 3–4. Church of Jesus Christ of Latter Day Saints.

Karleen, Paul S. *The Handbook to Bible Study: With a Guide to the Scofield Study System.* New York: Oxford University Press, 1987.

Kesler, Jay. "Being Holy, Being Human: Dealing with the Expectations of Ministry." *Christianity Today,* 1988: Col 13: 17–18.

Knowles, Andre. *The Bible Guide,* 1st Augsburg Books, ed. Minneapolis, MN: Augsburg, 2001.

Kreeft, Peter. *Fundamentals of the Faith: Essays in Christian Apologetics.* San Francisco, CA: Ignatius Press, 1988.

Lewis, C. S. *Mere Christianity.* New York: Harper One, 1952.

Lightner, Robert P. "Phillipians." In *The Bible Knowledge Commentary: An Exposition of the Scriptures,* ed. Wheaton, IL: Victor Books, 1985.

Lloyd-Jones, D. M. *Darkness and Light: An Exposition of Ephesians 4:17–5:17.* Carlyle, PA: Banner of Truth, 1982.

———. *God the Holy Spirit.* Wheaton, IL: Crossway Books, 1997.

Lucado, Max, and Randy Frazee. *The Story NIV.* Grand Rapids, MI: Zondervan, 2011.

Luther, Martin. *The Freedom of a Christian, MLS: 71–80.*

Lyndon, John. *From Sacrifice to Sacrament: Repentace in A Christian Context.* Nanham, NY: Rowan and Littlefield: Logos, 1977.

MacArthur, John F. *Rediscovering Expository Preaching.* Dallas, TX: Word Publishing, 1992.

MacArthur, John. *Twelve Ordinary Men.* Nashville, TN: Thomas Nelson, 2002.

Manser, Martin H. *Dictionary of Bible Themes: The Accessible and Comprehensive Tool for Topical Studies.* London: Martin Manser: Logos, 2009.

Martin, Dr. Walter. *Kingdom of the Cults.* Grand Rapids, MI: Bethany House, 1977.

McCracken. *Grey Matter.* Grand Rapids, MI: Baker Books, 2013.

McDonald, W. For Holiness or Anitnomianism Revived; Introduction. eugene Oregon: Wipf and Stock Publishers, 1889.

Mcgee, J. Vernon. http://www.oneplace.com/ministries/thru-the-bible-with-j-vernon-mcgree/.

MCKee, Miles. *Jesus Is God: He Always Was and Always Will be.* Kindle ed.

McKnight, Scott. *A Fellowship of Differents.* Zondervan, 2015.

McQuilkin, Robertson. *The Keswick Perspective: Five Views on Sanctification.* Grand Rapids, MI: Zondervan, 1987.

Merriam-Webster, *Merriam-Webster's Collegiate Dictionary., 11th ed.* Springfield, MA: Merriam-Webster, 2003.

Merrill, Eugene H. "The Pentateuch." In *Holman Concise*, by David S. Dockery. Nashville, TN: Broadman and Holman, 1996.

Mills, M. S. *The Life of Christ: A Study Guide to the Gospel Record*. Dallas, TX: 3E Minitstries, 199.

Morey, Robert A. *Studies In the Atonement*. Orange, CA: Christian Scholars Press, 2007.

Murray, John. "Principles of Conduct." In *Five Views of Law and Gospel*, ed. Stanley N. Gundry. Grand Rapids, MI: Zondervan, 1996.

Nelson, P. C. *Bible Doctrines*. Springfield, MO: Gospel Publishing, 1948.

O'Donovan, Oliver. *Ressurection and Moral Order: An Outline for Evangelical Ethics*. Leicester: Apollos, 1996.

Oluwasina E. Oluwaleke. *Bearing the Fruits of the Kingdom of God*. Lagos, Nigeria: Christos Ambassadors Ministries. 2017

Osbeck, Kenneth W. *Amazing Grace: 366 Inspiring Hymn Stories for Daily Devotions. Trust and Obey by John H. Sammis (1846–1919)*. Grand Rapids, MI: Kregel, 1996.

Owen, John. *Temptation and Sin*. Lafayette, IN: Sovereign Grace Publishing, 2001.

———. *The Holy Spirit*. Carlisle, PA: Banner of Truth, 1965.

Packer, J. I. *Concise Theology: A Guide to Historic Christian Beliefs*. Wheaton, IL: Tyndale House: Logos, 1993.

———. *Growing in Christ*. Wheaton, IL: Crossway Books, 1994.

———. *Knowing God*. Downers Grove, IL: Intra-Varsity Press, 1973.

Pawson, David. *Once Saved, Always Saved: A Study in Perserverance and Inheritance*. London: Hodder & Sloughton, 1996.

Pearlman, Myer. *Knowing the Doctrines of the Bible*. Springfield, MO: Gospel Publishing, 1937.

Pearson, Nancy. *Total Truth: Liberating Christianity from Its Cultural Captivity*. Wheaton, IL: Crossway Books, 2005.

Peterson, Eugene H. *A Long Obedience in the Same Direction: Discipleship in an Instant Society.* 2nd ed. Downers Grove, IL: IVP Books, 2000.

Pickett, Fuchsia. *Five Laws of the Dying Seed: Discover the Secret to a Fruitful Life.* Lake Mary, FL: Charisma House, 2003.

Pratney, W. A. *The Nature And Character of God.* Minneapolis, MN: Bethany House, 1988.

Quanstrom, Mark A. *From Grace to Grace.* Kansas City, MO: Beacon Hill, 2011.

quote, John Owens. *Go and Sin No More. p, 95.* Regal Books, 1999.

Rewinkel, Alfred M. *The Flood: In Light of Geology and Archaelogy.* St. Louis, MO: Concordia Publishing, 1951.

Ritchie, Rick. "What is This Law and Gospel Thing?" *Modern Reformation*, March/April 1993: 7–11.

Roberts, Richard Owen. *Repentance: The First Word of the Gospel.* Wheaton, IL: Crossway, 2002.

Ryle, J. C. "Holiness: Its Nature, Hindances, Difficulties, and Roots." Light by Design. net: Kindle Books.

Ryrie, Charles Caldwell. *A Survey of Bible Doctrine.* Chicago: Moody Press, 1972.

Steele, Daniel. *For Holiness or Antinomianism, Revised: The Theology of the So-Called Plymouth Brethren Examined and Refuted.* Christian Witness Publishing, Kindle location 285, 1899.

Saunders, E. P. *Paul And Palestinian Judaism: A Comparison of Patterns of Religion.* Minneapolis, MN: Fortress Press, 2017.

Schaeffer, Francis. *He Is There and He Is Not Silent.* London: Hodder and Stroughton, 1972.

Schneider, Johann. "Agricola." In *Who's Who in Christian History*, ed. J.D. Douglass and Philip W. Comfort. Wheaton, IL: Tyndale House, 1992.

Schreiner, T. R. "In the New Testament." In *New Bible Dictionary*, ed. I. H. Marshall, A. R. Millard, et al., D. R. W. Wood. Leicester, England: Downers Grove, IL: InterVarsity Press, 1996.

Servant, David A. *The Great Gospel Deception: Exposing the False Promise of Heaven Without Holiness.* epub edition (Kindle) ISBN: 978-1-939788-90-0, 1999.

Shedd, William G. T. *Dogmatic Theology.* 3rd ed. Phillipsburg, NJ: Presbyterian & Reformed Publishing, 2003.

Sire, W. James. *Naming the Elephant.* Downers Grove, IL: InterVarsity Press, 2004.

Sproul, R. C. *The Holiness of God.* Tyndale House, 1985.

————. *What Is Repentance?* Sanford, FL: Reformation Trust, 2014.

————. *www. ligonier.org.* www.ligonier.org/learn/series/holiness_of_God/the_importance-of-holiness/? (accessed 2017).

Spurgeon, Charles. *Holiness Demanded.* www.//http. puritandownloads.com (accessed 2016).

Stanley, Charles. In Touch Ministries.

Stephenson, Lester L. *A Biblicist View of the Law and Gospel.* Greenville, SC: Ambassador Int, Kindle ed., 2017

Story, Dan. *Defending Your Faith.* Grand Rapids, MI: Kregel Publications, 1997.

Strom, Andrew. *True and False Revival.* Revival School Publishers, 2008.

Strong, James. *A Concise Distonary of the Words in the Greek Testament and the Hebrew Bible.* Bellingham, WA: Logos Bible Software, 2009.

————. *The New Strong's Exhaustive Concordance of the Bible.* Nashville, TN: Thomas Nelson 1996.

Swindoll, Charles, and Roy B. Zuck. *Understand Christian Theology.* Nashville, TN: Thomas Nelson, 2003.

Kreeft, Peter, and Ronald K. Tacelli *Handbook of Chritian Apologetics.* Downers Grove, Ill: Intervarsity Press, 1994.

Tan, Paul Lee. "Signs of the Times." In *Encyclopedia of 7700 Illustrations.* Garland, TX: Bible Communications, 1996.

Torrey, R. A. *The Deity of Jesus Christ.* Kindle ed., 1856–1928.

————. *The New Topical Textbook: A Scriptural Text Book for the Use of Ministers, Teachers, and All Christian Workers.* Oak Harbor, WA: Logos Research Systems, 2001.

Torrence, Thomas F. *Theological Studies.* New York: Oxford University Press. 1969.

Toussaint, Stanley D. "Acts." In *The Bible Knowledge Commentary: An Expositionof the Scritpures,* ed. J. F. Walvoord and R. B. Tuck, Acts 15:19–35. Wheaton, IL: Victor Books, 1985.

Tozer, A. W. *The Knowledge of the Holy: The Attributes of God.* New York: Harper Collins, 1897–1963.

Turabian, Kate L. *A Manual for Writers of Research Papers, Theses, and Dissertations,* 7th ed. Chicago, IL: University of Chicago Press, 2003.

Tyson, John R. ED. Charles Wesley: A Reader. New York: Oxford, 1989.

Utley, Robert James. *Paul's Fourth Missionary Journey: 1 Timothy, Titus, II Timothy.* Study Guide Commentary Series, vol. 9. Marshall, TX: Bible Lessons International: Logos, 200.

————. *The Beloved Disciple's Memoirs and Letters: The Gospel of John, I II and III John.* Study Guide Commentary Series, vol. 4. Marshall, TX: Bible Lessons International, 1999.

VanGemeren, William A. *Five Views on the Law and the Gospel.* Grand Rapids, MI: Zondervan, 1996.

Vaugn, Rev. C. J. Suggestive thoughts: half-hours in the Temple church.

Kaiser, Walter C. Jr. "As God's gracious guidance for the Promotion of Holiness." In *Five Views on Law and Gospel.* Grand Rapids, MI: Zondervan, 1996.

Watson, Thomas. *A Body of Divinity.* Google books, 147.

Weisbe, Warren B. *Be Holy.* "Be" Commentary Series. Wheaton, IL: Victor Books, Logos, 1996.

Wesley, John. *Sermons, on Several Occasions.* Oak Harbor, WA: Logos Research Systems, 1999.

————. *WJW 5:223–33 & WJW 5:144–46.*

Wesley, Rev. John. *A Plain Account of Christian Perfection: As believed and taught by Rev. Mr. John Wesley, from the years 1725–1777.* Grand Rapids, MI: Baker, 1986.

Whitefield, George. *Selected Sermons of George Whitefield.* Oak Harbor, WA: Logos Edition, 1999.

Williams, A. Lukyn. "Matthew." Vol 1" in *Pulpit Commentary, ed.* Spense & Joseph Exell. New York: Funk and Wagnell, 1913.

Young, Kevin De. "A Catholic Laments the Evangelical Sin of Biblicism." *Christian Research Journal* 35, no. 2, 2012.

Zacharius, Ravi. Quoted from statement on radio broadcast, 2018.

Zornes, Ben. *The Fruitful Christian Life: Meditations of the Fruit of the Spirit.* Windsor, CO: Ellerslie Press, 2014. Kindle edition.

Printed in the United States
By Bookmasters